ART AND THE
CHRISTIAN MIND

the life and work of H. R. Rookmaaker

LAUREL GASQUE

CROSSWAY BOOKS

A PUBLISHING MINISTRY OF
GOOD NEWS PUBLISHERS
WHEATON, ILLINOIS

Art and the Christian Mind

Originally published by Piquant, Carlisle, United Kingdom in *The Complete Works of H.R. Rookmaaker*, Part 4, Volume 6: "Hans Rookmaaker: An Open Life," copyright © 2003.

Copyright © 2005 by Laurel Gasque

Published by Crossway Books
        A publishing ministry of Good News Publishers
        1300 Crescent Street
        Wheaton, Illinois 60187

Cover design: Jon McGrath

Cover photo: Getty Images

First printing, 2005

Printed in the United States of America

All photographs are used by permission of Marleen Hengelaar-Rookmaaker.

Library of Congress Cataloging-in-Publication Data
Gasque, Laurel, 1942–
    Art and the Christian mind : the life and work of H. R. Rookmaaker / Laurel Gasque.
      p. cm.
    ISBN 1-58134-694-8 (tpb)
    1. Rookmaaker, H. R. (Hendrik Roelof), 1922-1977. 2. Reformed (Reformed Church)—Netherlands—Biography. 3. Art historians—Netherlands—Biography. I. Title.
BX9479.R66G37   2005
284'.2'092—dc22   2005003663

VP		15	14	13	12	11	10	09	08	07	06	05
15	14	13	12	11	10	9	8	7	6	5	4	3	2	1

CONTENTS

PREFACE

In the spring of 1977 I was living in Edinburgh. The sun was shining beautifully through the windowpanes of my little flat on Rose Street when I answered the telephone on Monday, March 14. My delight in the day and at hearing Marleen Rookmaaker's voice soon jolted into a dark shadow of shock and sadness as she told me that her father had died in the early evening of the night before. It hardly seemed possible that he could have slipped away from all of us so suddenly.

Sorrow softened as I listened to Bach's wonderful cantata, *Gottes Zeit is die allerbeste Zeit* (BWV 106): "God's time is the very best time. . . . In him, we die at the right time, as he wills." Then memories flooded in.

My husband, Ward, and I treasured our friendship with Hans. There had been so many memorable and enjoyable times with him and with Anky and the family. We had had opportunity to see him in all sorts of surroundings: in the intimacy of our home in Vancouver on extended visits as our houseguest, at Dutch and Swiss L'Abri, as well as in various British, American, and Austrian settings. Publicly and personally, professionally and privately, there was no contradiction. He was completely himself. He did not try to ingratiate himself through small talk or chitchat. But he did have a great sense of humor. I think Ward is the only person I ever saw who could make him laugh heartily at himself. We loved the fact that he did not take himself seriously every second of the day.

We also almost killed ourselves suppressing our laughter on one occasion at seeing Hans trying to be as tactful as possible in giving his opinion of a work of art in which one of our colleagues had invested a considerable amount of money despite his wife's disapproval. He was obviously looking for Hans's endorsement to justify his expenditure and confirm his good taste. When Hans was not immediately forthcoming, he finally asked, "What do you think?" There was a significant interval of silence. There we all were, including our colleague and his spouse and children, waiting with bated breath to hear Hans's expert opinion. Fiddling with his pipe a bit, he finally looked around at all of us and then at the painting and said, "Well, it really should be entitled, 'Tunnel of Love.' It would be best if you put it under your bed."

But writing the biography of a mentor and friend is not simply about warm personal reminiscences. Over the course of writing this brief biography, I have had to ask myself many questions about what it means to give a textual account of someone's life with fidelity to the remaining documentary evidence as well as to the highly personal memories (including my own) of those still living.

By turns I have been challenged, humbled, and awed by the life of a person who was neither famous nor obscure by worldly standards. Here was someone who lived a relatively ordinary life of influence in the middle of the twentieth century. The upsurge in biography today often goes hand in hand with catering to curiosity about a celebrity and the hunger of the public to know the foibles of a famous person's life. Few famous people in any age can be what one might call typical of their time.

Yet we desire deeply to know the lives of people and long for figures who represent their ages. Perhaps the main reason the Bible is still the world's best seller and we name so many of our children after its cast of characters is that it is a book of biographies, giving powerfully rendered, unvarnished, and distilled lives of people who made a difference for good or ill.

Biographies help give us our moral place in history as we participate through identification with or reaction against those about whom we read. Biographies also overcome the arbitrary distinctions and artificial divisions we make when thinking or writing about history. At best, if crafted well, they can synthesize a personal perspective with a wider view of the events of a period that inspires us to try to understand another time or to live well in the present.

The struggle to achieve a moving narrative while remaining faithful to written evidence and personal recollections is not easy. It provides a great temptation for the biographer to move subtly to create a form closer to fiction than the more limited telling of a life based almost strictly on what can be corroborated.

Out of complete sincerity and desire for Hans Rookmaaker's name not to fall into oblivion, the late Linette Martin made an important first attempt to share his life soon after he died by publishing a biography in 1979. For that, anyone who values the life and work of H.R. Rookmaaker must be grateful. Despite inconsistency regarding chronology, some historical inaccuracies, and elements of invented narrative, anyone who writes a biography after her work stands on her shoulders and owes her a debt of appreciation. In the latter part of her book, she was able brilliantly to capture Rookmaaker's colloquially voiced speech on a page of written text—a voice we do not hear in quite the same way in his recorded lectures or his letters. It is so authentic that we can ever be grateful for her dramatist's gift and forgive her for her factual errors.

The purpose of this additional biography has been to link Rookmaaker to his works and his ongoing influence as well as to try to correct a number of inaccuracies. There has also been an attempt to elaborate the important influence of some people and perspectives in shaping his life and outlook that were overlooked previously.

In his own right, the life and thought of J.P.A. Mekkes, Rookmaaker's most important mentor and a key post-World War II Dutch Reformational thinker, still needs to be made available to English-speaking audiences. Further reflection on the relationship of Hans Rookmaaker and Francis Schaeffer in their missional dynamic to the so-called hippie generation would also be helpful. It would also be useful for a historian of Christianity to explore the bridge between Rookmaaker's life and thought and the current generation who have been influenced by him in their art or thinking or written work.

I am more than painfully aware of many names that are missing from this account of the life and influence of Hans Rookmaaker that could be mentioned. No biography can encompass a whole life. The next biographer perhaps can craft it even more inclusively now that we have the published *Complete Works* available in accessible form.

I am reminded of Hans's playfulness. Walking along a sidewalk with his family and with our family, he would rush ahead of all of us and say, "Three steps forward and two steps back!" and have us all doing the same thing down the street as people looked at us as if we were crazy. What a life lesson in hope! There are setbacks, but buck up—we are also, by God's grace, going forward. At many instances along the way in life and work, and as I wrote this biography, I have been reminded of "three steps forward and two steps back," not by abstract admonition but by the remembrance of the act of charging up and down an ordinary street in a normal neighborhood, three steps forward and two steps back.

No biography can get it all right. The aim of this biography has been simply to say that an "ordinary" life can make an extraordinary difference.

ACKNOWLEDGMENTS

First and foremost, I would like to acknowledge my deep gratitude to the subject of this biography. Hans Rookmaaker never failed to encourage me intellectually and spiritually through friendship or to inspire me to independence of vocation by his creative example and serious conversation. Through his generous gift of time in viewing art and architecture, listening to music, and discussing vigorously, extensively, and openly issues of culture and meaning with me, he gave a dimension to my education that I could never have obtained by formal means. Hans's complete confidence in the indissoluble relation between art and reality and his wise understanding of their interrelatedness have enriched my thinking and, indeed, my life.

It has been an honor and privilege to write this brief biography of someone who has contributed so much to so many lives, including my own. For this invitation I thank Marleen Hengelaar-Rookmaaker and Pieter Kwant. I am humbled by the confidence they have placed in me to undertake this task.

I have benefited greatly from the generosity and trust of the Rookmaaker family in allowing me to have access to family records, documents, letters, and photos, as well as Hans Rookmaaker's annual appointment agendas. Sadly, Anky Rookmaaker died on February 10, 2003, as this account of her husband's life was being completed. Throughout the process of research and verifying details, she kindly assisted as she could until only a few weeks before her death. I shall always appreciate the extended interview I was able to have with her in July

2001 in Ommen, her welcome then, and her hospitality on many other occasions. I also value the opportunity I had many years ago to meet both of Hans's sisters, Door Haver Droeze and Hannie Rotgans, who were my dinner partners at a family occasion I was invited to join. Less than a year before her death in 2002, Hannie allowed me to interview her in her home in The Hague. Door passed away in 1989.

Again, I give my thanks to Marleen Hengelaar-Rookmaaker. She has been patient beyond measure and indefatigable in answering questions and tracking down or correcting information for me. I am grateful for help with the history of Redt een Kind (Save a Child) from her husband, Albert Hengelaar. I am also appreciative of their gracious hospitality and extraordinary helpfulness when I have been in the Netherlands. Their warm friendship has heartened me at every stage of my work.

Special thanks must go to Jaco Bauer for her unwavering help in translating many documents and letters from Dutch. Her grace and good humor during long hours of working together have sustained me when I thought we might not ever get through some materials.

The staff of the Special Collections of the Buswell Memorial Library at Wheaton College (Wheaton, Illinois, USA)—David Malone, Head of Special Collections and College Archivist; David Osielski, Reference Archivist; and Keith Call, Assistant Archivist—are all owed my thanks for their outstanding help as I worked through the Hans Rookmaaker Papers in their custody. I am also indebted to Graham Birtwistle and C.A. van Swigchem of the Free University of Amsterdam for a record of the history of the Department of Art History. I thank Graham Birtwistle for answering many other inquiries as well.

I would like to extend my appreciation for photographs appearing in this biography taken by Sylvester Jacobs, John Walford, and Peter Smith. I also gratefully acknowledge the help of the Documentatiecentrum at the Free University in tracing photographic material.

Many, many people have openheartedly shared their memories with me or openhandedly assisted me with valuable information in this project. I am sincerely grateful for their help. They are: the late David Alexander, Pat Alexander, Chris Anderson, Philip Archer, Thena Ayres, Jeremy Begbie, Elaine Botha, Ned Bustard, Raelene Cameron, Bettina and David Clowney, Tyrus Clutter, Eleanor DeLorme, Meryl Doney, Harry van Dyke, Bill and Grace Dyrness, Joyce Erickson, Eduardo Escheverria, Lindsay Farrell, Roger Feldman, David and Susan Fetcho, Don Forsythe, Rudi Fuchs, Sharon Gallagher, Nigel Goodwin, Erica Grimm-Vance, David Hanson, Bruce Herman, Irving Hexham, Eugene Johnson, Marc de Klijn, Jason Knapp, Ed Knippers, Roel Kuiper, George Langbroek, Barbara Lidfors, Ranald and Susan Macaulay, Mary Leigh Morbey, David Muir, Karen Mulder, Laurie Nelson, Gerard Pas, Albert Pedulla, Ted and Cathy Prescott, David Porter, Wayne Roosa, Dan Russ, Phil Schaafsma, Edith Schaeffer, Dal and Kit Schindell, Rachel Smith, Betty Spackman, Frank Speyers, T. Grady Spires, Barbara and Jonathan Stanfield, Alva Steffler, Norman Stone, Charles Twombly, Maria Walford-Dellù, Murray Watts, Graham Weeks, and Shorty Yeaworth.

Many friends and colleagues sustained me during this endeavor in ways that defy categories that I have already mentioned. I wish to acknowledge their support. Friends who have been at my side are: Joy Gratz, Pat Henneman, Mary Frank, Julia Popp, Chris and Jeannie Houston, John and Debbie Bowen, Don and Maureen Bennett, Ruth and Ken Smith, Jerry and Jane Hawthorne, Susan and Steve Phillips, David and Lucia Gill, Don and Edie Tinder, Leona DeFehr, Jim and Diane Alimena, Elizabeth and Jim Gladden, Bob and Julie Fredericks, Peter and Frances Shaw, Ruth and Paul Pitt, John and Babby Schwarz, Grace Irwin, Janet and Jeff Greenman, Brian and Lily Stiller, Ruth Ericson Byrholdt, Betty Bennett, Soo Inn Tan, Earl Palmer, Luci Shaw, and Greg Wolfe. I would like to give particular thanks to some of my International Fellowship of Evangelical Students (IFES) and Inter-Varsity Christian Fellowship of Canada colleagues who have encouraged me to write: Lindsay and Ann Brown, Jim Berney,

Barb Boyt, and C.P.S. (Pat) Taylor. The solidarity of these friends and colleagues has been an enormous encouragement.

Elria Kwant, my constant communicant with Piquant, the British publisher, has been wonderful in helping me bring this biography to birth. The depth and breadth of her spirit in prodding me on has been singular. She has been the skilled midwife in bringing this book to life. I give her my heartfelt thanks for her perseverance throughout the long labor.

Last but not least, I would like to thank my dear, long-suffering family for all their care. Though I have been tense to live with at times, they have more than tolerated me and lived good-naturally with Hans as an adopted member of our family as I have written a narrative of his life. I thank my mother, Doris Sandfor, who lives in our home, for many a delicious dinner that took me away from obsessively thinking about the next sentence I should write to family fellowship and a wider perspective.

Many times while writing I have thought of my daughter, Michelle Gasque, as a small child giving Hans Rookmaaker a very respectful and wide berth as she encountered him, especially going up or down the stairs. She was not exactly afraid of him, but she knew instinctively as a child that he was not someone to fawn over small children. This probably left a much more distinct trace on her memory of him than of the many houseguests in our home who tried to sidle up to her. She has cheered me on from the outset and cared for me touchingly all along the way.

To my husband, Ward Gasque, I express deepest thanks for all his skilled help and sound advice, from dealing with the smallest detail to taking in an understanding of the whole scope of the task in which I was involved. Words can hardly convey the depth of appreciation and feeling I have for his constancy and care and concern that I bring my work to completion well.

Laurel Gasque
Camano Island, Washington, 2003

ONE

IMPACT

Hans Rookmaaker's life spanned a mere fifty-five years (1922–1977). Those years were situated symmetrically in the midst of the twentieth century. He completed the first half of the course of his life in 1949/1950. He was gone by 1977.

Since his death the arts scene among Christians of almost all traditions and denominations in Europe and North America has changed significantly. The Bible Society in New York City now has a serious art gallery. The National Gallery in London marked the year 2000 with an extraordinary exhibition of images of Christ sponsored by two major trusts willing to back such an arts event despite the considerable embarrassment that some art historians still seem to have about Christian subject matter. Over the past thirty years Christian rock music has matured considerably lyrically and musically. Christians in the Visual Arts (CIVA) is an established organization linking and creatively supporting a wide network of Christian artists in all fields of the visual arts. *Image: A Journal of the Arts & Religion* serves as a beacon of hope for many writers and artists as it speaks credibly from a perspective of faith-commitment to a wider culture beyond the boundaries of religious institutions. In Scotland the Leith School of Art was founded, and in the Netherlands a Christian art academy was established as a result of Rookmaaker's own efforts.

A generation ago these kinds of developments and resources that we have begun to take for granted simply did not exist. In North America the marginalizing and minimizing of the arts were not just a condition of the church but also of a pragmatic culture that viewed the arts as a luxury rather than a necessity. In Europe the situation was different. The wider culture valued the arts and invested in them more than their North American counterparts. For many cultured Europeans art, filled with the beauty and greatness of past human achievement, was a surrogate religion. For an extremely influential and highly intellectual minority, it became a staging ground for raging anger and discontent, especially after the debacle of World War II and the collapse of confidence in an abiding moral order. On both sides of the Atlantic the church, challenged by a new society and not completely confident of its identity, frequently closed its eyes and ears to culture by ignoring trends or becoming defensive.

With extraordinary openness and human sympathy, and with deep faith, Hans Rookmaaker faced these cultural conditions squarely. Not only did many of the arts developments mentioned above not exist a generation ago, but they were not fully imaginable. The dynamic impact of Rookmaaker's life and his short lifework made them a lot more probable. Out of all proportion to his length of days, he qualitatively influenced key individuals and groups that would have a remarkable effect on changing attitudes toward the arts in the church and many other institutions.

In 1961 at the height of the Cold War and the great race for space between the Soviets and the Americans, Rookmaaker, not yet a full professor but teaching at the University of Leiden, made his first extended trip to North America. He was not sponsored or invited by churches, though individual friends from his Reformed tradition welcomed him and warmly hosted him, but came through a grant funded by the Dutch government. The purpose of his trip was to make a study of the teaching of art history in the United States.

To say the least, he made the most of this trip. While in the United States he visited virtually every major center of art-historical study east of St. Louis as well as every major art collection from the northeast seaboard to the Midwest. He attended the College Art Association meeting in New York City, where he met many prominent art historians. He took this golden opportunity also to pursue his passion for African-American music and culture. By this time he was an expert in this field and had recently published a book on jazz, blues, and spirituals. His diary during this trip is dotted with contacts with leading black figures such as Thomas A. Dorsey, Mahalia Jackson, and Langston Hughes. Furthermore, he managed to meet a wide range of church-affiliated people, from black Baptists and Dutch Reformed types to a broad spectrum of evangelicals attached to institutions such as Calvin College and Wheaton College and organizations such as Christianity Today. He also traveled to Canada. Afterward he exuberantly corresponded with an amazing number of the people he had met on his travels.

Rookmaaker continued to deepen his thought and nurture his friendships. By 1968 he was a professor and had formed the Art History Department of the Free University of Amsterdam. He was in full stride. The intervening years had helped prepare him for an increasingly chaotic culture. Often this period is looked back at nostalgically as a gentler, more peace-loving time flowing with flower children and happy hippies, when marijuana filled the air and some social issues, such as basic civil rights for blacks in the USA, got straightened out. With fading memory the fierceness of the student protest movements that were gaining strength both in Europe and North America have not always remained clear. When a U.S. combat troop led by Lieutenant William Calley massacred all five hundred civilians of the Vietnamese village of My Lai though they showed no sign of resistance, that tragedy inflamed intense anger, as did the entire war. The attempted assassination of Rudi Dutschke, a well-known German student anarchist and activist, unleashed turbulent solidarity demonstrations in Vienna, Paris, Rome, and London. Student protests closed down the University of Paris in the spring of 1968 and turned the streets of Paris into a battle zone, imperiling the government. West Germany was launched into a decade of tumultuous internal struggle as radicals gathering around the Baader-Meinhof Gang tried to kick-start revolution through violence and terrorism.

During these tumultuous years of student unrest in the late 1960s and early 1970s, few thinkers or leaders were prepared for the hard social, political, and philosophical realities of this era. Many academic and administrative careers were broken in universities across the world. Rookmaaker was not impervious to the pressures on and within his own institution or on himself as an administrator and teacher. But, remarkably, he was prepared spiritually and intellectually for the fundamental challenge of the younger generation's radical quest and the turbulence of the times it helped create, because through the years he had striven earnestly to bring to bear Christian understanding on all the issues of life. He made a huge impact on the lives of students in several countries.

At first glance he looked like an unlikely person to have much to say to a radical and rebellious generation bent on changing not only the university but also society and its mores. A driver's license that he obtained in 1961 during his extended travels in the USA describes him as having brown hair and eyes, weighing 160 pounds, with a height of five feet and eight inches. He was not physically a big man or imposing at all. Dressed in an English worsted three-piece suit and smoking his pipe, he appeared a typical, comfortably positioned bureaucrat or professor. He looked more like a bank manager than an art historian. There was not a trace of bohemian manner in his style. On the surface, it was not difficult to suspect him of being slightly out of touch with current trends or contemporary culture.

When the clamor came, however, he was ready. Many times he faced hostile audiences of art students who were astonished to hear this ordinary-looking, little professor talking impassionately and intelligently about contemporary issues and trends from a Christian perspective. His courage in facing and discussing the questions of art and morals in society, areas rarely ventured into publicly by conservative Christians, motivated many reluctant Christian students who had compartmentalized their lives to relate their faith to their whole lives and studies in a deep and lively way.

But it was not only Christian students who responded to him. Tony Wales, who in the mid-1960s served on the staff of British Inter-Varsity Fellowship (IVF), said he had seen students and others come to faith in Christ through such Rookmaaker lectures as "Three Steps to Modern Art." Wales also had seen him receive a standing ovation by several hundred students at a London art college following a two-hour-long presentation and analysis of rock and protest music. On that occasion not only did these students of the protest generation show their respect, but at the end of the same lecture the chairman of the painting department of the college acknowledged that he now for the first time could understand his own son. Wales also relates Rookmaaker's evident disappointment on another occasion when a lecture he was to give at the Royal Academy had to be moved to a larger hall because the Reynolds Room was bulging with people!

Rookmaaker was a masterful communicator in both Dutch and English. When the lights went down and he started to show slides of great works of art of the past or startling contemporary art and comment on them, his audience was fascinated, whether they agreed with him or not. His lecturing style was highly unusual for a continental professor, as he spoke not from a written manuscript but extemporaneously and with full attentive engagement with his listeners. It was an art form, a performance. Like a jazz musician playing inventively with themes, he would improvise within a given structure (the lecture topic) with mastery and control, skill and intensity. He would bait and shock, amuse and bemuse. A lot hung on the sequence of visual or audio examples he used. The more often he repeated a lecture, the richer it got. His material never became stale with repetition because there was always something new, if only in the provocative tone or way he put things.

In the light of day he was equally compelling. Going to an art gallery with him was an exceptional learning experience. He regularly took his own students from the Free University to the many special art collections in the Netherlands as well as on extended excursions to collections abroad, especially to Italy. But he also frequently invited small groups or individuals to join him at the art museum when he spoke at conferences.

He did not feel compelled to look at every painting or work of art when he entered a gallery. He would say, "Look at the one that draws you to itself." Or when he gathered a small group before a picture, he would ask the most obvious question first: "What are you looking at?" Often there was acute discomfort in the group because such a basic question seemed so self-evident. Suspicion would arise that there must be some hidden agenda behind it to expose their ignorance. Rookmaaker, however, never toyed with people in this way. He would be playful and provocative for pedagogical purposes. He was always a sincere teacher. Soon everyone in the little group would learn that they genuinely needed to see firsthand what they were looking at. Afterward this made Rookmaaker's own remarks on the picture all the more rewarding because everyone in the group had started first by seeing it for himself or herself.

Rookmaaker was protective of his little flock of students when visiting an art gallery. He did not take kindly to interlopers with whom he did not have a personal connection. Many of his students relate incidents when a curious visitor would sidle up to the group to hear the interesting things the small, dignified gentleman was saying only to be told directly by him in a not so gentle way, "This is a very special art history course. It costs two thousand dollars. Please go away!" Aghast, the intruder would leave. And the small group would beam at being considered so special and exclusive. There lurked beneath an unpretentious exterior a complex personality of immense vitality and not a few surprises.

Rookmaaker brought his own humanity and his understanding of humanity to his scholarship in a conscious way that is unusual for academics. He also sought to help his students bring their humanity fully into their learning and studies. His own words best describe how important the human element was for him in learning and teaching:

> We must judge as human beings, not as an abstract homo aestheticus, not as art historians or as artists but with our full human being. . . . But everyone may and can judge art. The difference comes between a practiced judgment, based on experience, and the judgment of someone who is just beginning to look. The latter must still learn a lot—in the first place, to see. And that is exactly the situation of our students. We also need to teach them to look as human beings. All of education is concerned with the humanity of young people. The point of departure is their humanity, their young and inexperienced humanity. They need to develop competence in judging, they need to gain experience and insight. They will have to do that themselves. It is all too subtle and too richly multicoloured for us to be able to teach it to them as one teaches a maths sum.

But we will have to show them the way. Help them. Pass on something of our experience and our knowledge by which they at least can be guarded from the most obvious misconceptions and dead ends. . . .

The student expects that you will judge as a human being . . . a person with conviction, a point of view, a person with a warm heart who can get angry and can also say why you were so moved or became so enthusiastic, can explain why something had such an impact on you. We may talk about works of art, preferably close to the works of art themselves, as long as it is not an argument for argument's sake—so interesting and so cultural—as long as the real commitment is to find the truth, to say the right thing, in order to do justice to the artist, the work in question, and to the students and ourselves as well.

Besides, we can be sure that our work is never perfect. But it certainly can be meaningful. It is possible to work and deal with art and with students in this way. If it were impossible, it would be better never to speak about art again, no, even stronger, to never look at it again. After all, the work proves to be humanly impossible to approach and does not really require our reaction, the input of our personality. Basically these things are about love for our neighbour and for the truth, because only these can make us free and make our work meaningful.(CW [Complete Works], 2:134–135)

In 1970, the year Rookmaaker published his best-selling book *Modern Art and the Death of a Culture*, most students in Europe or North America were not being thought of or educated in this deeply human and personal way. On May 4 that year, the world looked on with horror as students, only some of whom were protesters against the bombing of Cambodia (a decision by President Nixon that appeared to expand the Vietnam War), were gunned down by National Guardsmen on the campus of Kent State University in Kent, Ohio. The opening words of Rookmaaker's book perfectly captured the mood of the era: "We live at a time of great change, of protest and revolution. We are aware that something radical is happening around us, but it is not always easy to see just what it is" (*CW*, 5:5).

He was exactly on target. Rookmaaker had written a searing account in this work of the dehumanization of life in our times as shown in the rise of modern art. These were threatening words for many who had accommodated themselves comfortably to modernity and contemporary culture, whether they were or were not Christians, or whether they were or were not aware of this conformity. When it came out, *Modern Art and the Death of a Culture* received wide acknowledgment and even acclaim, from a brief notice and review in *Art News* to Malcolm Muggeridge's making it one of his *Observer* Books of the Year for 1970. Muggeridge also promoted it in *Esquire*, where he was also a book review editor. *Modern Art and the Death of a Culture* was a genuine crossover book. It used a single language that was accessible to people whether they had Christian conviction or not. Its success may possibly have inspired its copy-editor at Inter-Varsity Press in England, David Alexander, to co-found with his wife, Pat Alexander, Lion Publishing, a new press dedicated to a refreshingly inclusive way of communicating with and engaging the public.

In *Modern Art and the Death of a Culture*, Rookmaaker resolutely faced the problematic and polemical character of modern art that denounced the nature and dignity of humanity. In the nineteenth century Nietzsche said, "God is dead." In the twentieth century, the most potent stream of modern art implicitly said, "Man is dead." Rookmaaker asked the question:

What has become of people? Miró once painted a picture of a picture. He took a reproduction of a secondary seventeenth-century Dutch picture (it could just as well have been a Vermeer or a Rembrandt) and gave his own reinterpretation. Nothing is more telling. 'Man is dead,' it says. The absurd, the strange, the void, the irrationally horrible is there. The old picture is treated with humour, scorn . . . and devastating irony until nothing is left. As the image is destroyed, so too is man. (CW, 5:88)

For Rookmaaker this was spiritual combat, not simply a matter of aesthetic niceties or opinions. He was attempting to awaken spiritual sleepers to the idea that modern art was not amoral or neutral but was loaded with meaning that conveyed an impact on all of us, whether we ever darkened the door of an art museum or not, because it was an assault on our humanity. The implications were not theoretical but were as practical as how we raise our children, elect our leaders, or care for the earth's environment.

A tremendous disruption with past assumptions of Western culture regarding the nature of humankind and reality had been heralded while most people were distracted by the clever allurements of a technological age. Modern artists like Picasso, Miró, and Duchamp not only promulgated a view of human beings as absurd but also celebrated it, led the way, and propagated it through their works of art. It is widely known that early audiences of this art reacted violently to it. This did not come generally from an informed perspective but out of an intuition at some vague level of being threatened. We may smile at their reaction to the shock of the new and feel mildly superior in being able now to appreciate this art. But Rookmaaker pointed out that only those practicing an aesthetic of detachment, interested purely in formal analysis of the work of art, or somewhat naive viewers not desiring to appear to be philistines could say, "The new art gives nothing more than a human message, conveyed by new means . . . [or] artists are expressing their times, and when they live in different times their forms are different."

He remarked further that "all the while the sometimes obvious content is being ignored. And even when there is an attempt to discuss content, they make it subjective and say 'This is how things are seen by this person.' In any event, to question the truth of what is stated in art is taboo" (CW, 5:196). Rookmaaker tackled both the radical implications of meaning in modern art and the studied refusal to engage that meaning.

This changing view of human beings, of course, did not happen overnight, or even in the decades at the turn of the twentieth century. Rookmaaker's own doctoral dissertation on Paul Gauguin, perhaps his most influential scholarly work, concentrated on this pivotal period at the turn of the century. However, his *Complete Works* attest that a monumental amount of his thinking went into analyzing and reflecting on the gradual transformation of thought regarding the nature of being human that transpired in Western culture since the time of the High Middle Ages. He focused frequently on views concerning human nature as formulated in Renaissance and Reformation thought during the sixteenth and seventeenth centuries, and particularly on the implications of the Enlightenment view of man in the eighteenth century for an unfolding view of modernity that the twentieth century ultimately received as a dubious legacy.

He forcefully engaged these ideas in his essay "Commitment in Art":

> This new vision of human beings and the world—a result of the development starting with the Enlightenment and continuing through Romanticism and positivism—was first given expression in painting. It happened around 1911: the old view of people having positive contact with reality, a contact already loosened by Impressionism, was totally destroyed. Human being [sic] as an absurdity, estranged from the world, which was in itself chaotic, accidental and apparently contingent and hostile, became the painter's new preoccupation. Some artists, like Picasso, began to paint absurd humanity, while others, like Kandinsky, turned to abstraction. In this revolution, this violent destruction of so many established values, much that was deeply anchored in the reality of human life was torn down. A great part of the alarmed public found it unacceptable. Just as people had reacted violently at the beginning of Impressionism, so Kandinsky relates how his abstract

paintings had to be cleaned every night at his exhibition in 1912 because the public had spat on his work. The artist was committed and had a message. That much the public accepted and did not deny, but being themselves also committed, they retained the right to reject that message. (CW, 5:192–193)

Rookmaaker's approach to these issues was not always appreciated and frequently stirred up strong reactions. Often he was (inaccurately, as his *Complete Works* attest) accused of not understanding and dismissing abstract art. He was criticized for focusing too much on the content and meaning of works of art. In an article written in 1972, Nicholas Wolterstorff believed that Rookmaaker looked "right through the sensory qualities of the work of art in order to discern the message beyond." Alva Steffler, an art professor at Wheaton College in Illinois, had a similar impression after reading Rookmaaker's writing and becoming personally acquainted with him in the early 1970s, though later modifying these views and coming to an appreciation of Rookmaaker's perspective.

No one may have put it in print, but there was a climate of criticism around Rookmaaker that regarded him as a popularizer. Rookmaaker's communication skills sympathetically won him nicknames like "the pipe-puffing pundit of Amsterdam" and "the Dutch Kenneth Clark" from some of his peers and colleagues. But in the academy there is often, unfortunately, a price to pay for the ability to communicate with a broad audience. Popularizing is not at all popular with most academics! The assumption is that doing this signifies that "the scholar" is "lightweight," meaning he or she is not sufficiently serious in undertaking scholarship. Such a person is frequently accused of oversimplifying complexities or even distorting issues for the sake of having an audience, whether this is well-founded or not. Both J.R.R. Tolkien and C.S. Lewis were ostracized to a certain extent by their Oxbridge colleagues because of this prejudice. Dorothy L. Sayers was not tarred with this brush because she was not and did not claim to be a scholar, though her actual achievements belie this. But if the accusation places one in the company of people like the former, it may well be a badge of honor.

Rookmaaker seems to have borne with this well. He had a high degree of personal confidence. While he appreciated the esteem of his colleagues, it does not appear that he had any craven need for their approval. One wonders what his own awareness of his students' appreciation of him was. Did he have any sense of how far some of these inchoate artists and art historians would take his words and work and be formed significantly by them? He clearly basked in their admiration. Perhaps this approbation acted as compensation.

The extent of Rookmaaker's intellectual interests were far broader than usual for an academic. In his own field of art history, his writing was not confined to one or two areas of investigation but ranged over the whole course of Western art. At the same time he published works on African-American music and spoke about various cultural issues on public radio. Moving easily from technical philosophy and scholarship to readable, popular journalism, he was what today we might call a natural-born public intellectual. Yet he never eschewed or disparaged technical scholarship. In his association with Professor H. van de Waal of the University of Leiden, he helped pioneer DIAL/Iconclass, the most important technical art-historical research tool of the twentieth century for comprehensively classifying art-historical subject matter.

Rookmaaker deployed a broad blend of interests and competencies dynamically. He spoke a good number of European languages and had a reading knowledge of several more. Academically his ability ranged from researching technical scholarship for specialists to communicating many of these findings to a general public. He did both with equal respect. In both speaking and writing he had considerable skill to captivate. None of this, however, was in his case an end in itself to create a brilliant career or to achieve acknowledgment, though he became a full professor and received recognition. From the moment he opened himself to fully embracing a biblical faith in Jesus Christ he was on a mission that motivated him until his last breath. The light shed into his life by the true Light of the world illuminated his vision and imbued him with an immense sense of being called to be fully human in a world created by the living God in accordance with his rich reality. Essentially Rookmaaker's aim was to share this fullness of life with others, not in a reductive or one-sided way but in a way that reflected the complexity and completeness of God's sustaining love in creation.

During his lifetime relatively few people who heard him or read his work knew much about the circumstances of his life or the hard-won way he had come to be a Christian. Occasionally he would share that he had come to Christ in a German prisoner-of-war camp. But it barely needed being stated explicitly, because anyone with ears to hear could tell no matter what topic Rookmaaker talked about they were encountering a powerful genuineness based on actual experience. This tacit undercurrent of strength through struggle permeated his style. Undoubtedly this authenticity was key to his impact on an unusually wide diversity of people. He was not everyone's cup of tea or a typical mass communicator. He was often playful and implied meaning in a way that encouraged his audience to form their understanding of what he was saying in a way that integrated their thinking with their feeling, but he did not strive to manipulate emotions.

One would expect an art historian to influence other art historians. And Rookmaaker did. What is less usual is for an art historian to have influence on many artists, including musicians and writers. But this Rookmaaker also did. It is rare for an art historian to make an impact on mature scholars and thinkers in other fields. Rookmaaker did this as well. In the 1970 Summer School of Regent College (Vancouver, Canada), the distinguished British biblical scholar F.F. Bruce, who taught along with Rookmaaker during that time, made clear his appreciation for the widening of his horizons as a result of listening to his Dutch colleague. David McKenna, an influential American Christian educator, while president of Seattle Pacific University, desired to come and study with Rookmaaker because he felt that his understanding of culture was compellingly important for an understanding of higher education in the contemporary world.

Most rare is it for an art historian to make an impact on ordinary people with no singular interest in art, scholarship, or education. Yet Rookmaaker quite often could communicate with people from a variety of walks of life because he was not an aesthete, and his aim was ultimately not simply to inform people about art but to share with others through art the fullness of life and the richness of reality that God created through his love. As a result of hearing or reading Rookmaaker, a sincere housewife could stunningly be awakened to her ingrained bourgeois sentimentality or a businessman suddenly see that it might be a good thing to plant some trees and to landscape his parking lot instead of just covering it over with asphalt and cement.

He might infuriate some people on occasion. He was not totally approachable. He would have been the last person on the planet to coo over a baby. He would never have made a politician, trying to get elected. He had his shortcomings and blind spots. He could be gruff. He sometimes became truly angry. Though he never especially sought conflict, he could face it. He passionately sought to do justice to the complexities of any issue, idea, opinion, or work of art or scholarship that he encountered. He hungered and thirsted for righteousness. He was not a plaster saint but a man of many complexities and hidden depths.

Hans Rookmaaker's life rang true to reality. He unfailingly engaged his contemporary listeners and readers in refreshing and interesting ways that accorded with the experience of living in the twentieth century. It is all the more of interest for us that so much of his thought is still accessible and has application and relevance for many of the challenges of life in the twenty-first century.

Why is this so? Who was Hans Rookmaaker? What formed him?

As we follow the course of his life in subsequent chapters, these are the questions to be engaged.

TWO

CHILDHOOD

Henderik (Hans was his family nickname) Roelof Rookmaaker was born in The Hague, Netherlands, on February 27, 1922, an ominous year for what would transpire in the next decades for both Europe as a whole and for H.R. Rookmaaker personally. In that year Benito Mussolini came to power in Italy and remained so until 1943. The Weimar Republic was extremely fragile, stricken by soaring inflation and shaken in the following year by a threatened coup in Saxony and Thuringia, an uprising in Hamburg, and the infamous putsch that Adolf Hitler and his Nazi thugs attempted to stage in Munich. In 1922 the Union of Soviet Socialist Republics officially became federated under a plan drawn up by Joseph Stalin, the general secretary of the Communist Party at that time.

The post-World War I situation of the Netherlands was not especially stable either. Disputed territorial claims, economic crisis, kaleidoscopic shifting structures of political parties and their changing alliances with one another all contributed to numerous governments being formed up until the Nazi occupation of the country in the spring of 1940.

During this period while Germany was heading toward the Third Reich, the huge Dutch colony in Southeast Asia, the Dutch Indies (Indonesia's official name at that time), was heading for a showdown with its colonial masters in a struggle to gain national independence.

In the year of Hans Rookmaaker's birth, his father was in Holland on study leave from his post in the Dutch colonial service. For the previous five years he had served as a Controleur of the subdivision of Boné in the town of Watamponé in the southern part of Celebes (today Sulawesi). During the years 1920–1923 he eagerly elected to improve his administrative skills by opting for a two-year course offered at the newly created Dutch Indies Administration Academy (Nederlandsch-Indonesische Bestuursacademie) in The Hague.

Henderik Roelof Rookmaaker, Senior was born on August 21, 1887 in Batavia, the Dutch Indies (today Jakarta, Indonesia). His father before him, also a Henderik Roelof Rookmaaker (1848–1905), was also a colonial administrator in the Dutch East Indies and attained the office of Assistant-Resident.

A calligraphically designed family tree indicates nine Rookmaaker children born in the late nineteenth century in different places in the Dutch Indies as the Assistant-Resident and his, presumably, long-suffering wife traipsed from post to post around the Spice Islands to work and to live. Hans's father was the eighth child, and the third of four sons. He would surpass his father professionally by taking up the position of a full Resident (the highest administrative office in a major government district).

Theodora Catharina Heitink, Hans's mother, was born on March 17, 1890 in The Hague. As far as we know, she had no family links with the Dutch Indies. She was pretty. By family accounts she came from a good but not particularly religious family. As her husband also did not come from a religious background, that may have proved to be one of the most important similarities and perhaps one of the few things they genuinely had in common.

After graduating on June 20, 1911 from the University of Leiden, where he had studied in preparation for administrative service in the East Indies, Henderik married Theodora later that summer on August 25. By October of that year he was back in the East with his newly wedded wife and stationed at Pompanua in southern Celebes. The groom may have returned home to the land of his birth, but not so his bride. The adjustment that the two of them, still in their early twenties, had to make to each other and to living as a recently married couple in a culture so radically different from what Theodora had known before was considerable. It seems that she never fully adapted to living in this part of the world.

Soon children were to come. Theodora Catharina (nicknamed Door) was born on November 28, 1912, a little over a year after their arrival in Pompanua. Then two years later Henrietta Christina (nicknamed Hannie) was born on March 3, 1914. By this time Henderik was a Controller of South Boné in Mareq in another part of southern Celebes. He and Theodora were starting to continue the pattern of his peripatetic family of moving every one or two or few years in order to take up another colonial administrative position somewhere in this vast archipelago spreading itself from the Indian to the Pacific oceans.

In 1920, after nine years of marriage and living in the Dutch Indies, the Rookmaakers, now with two little girls of eight and six years old respectively, set out to return to the Netherlands. They made the most of their journey, taking five months and visiting China, Japan, and the United States on the way. The exquisite charm and beauty of Japanese gardens made a notable impression on Henderik. While we do not know what impressions her travels made on her, Theodora must have greatly anticipated and desired to be back in the land of her birth, where she could resume a way of life she found familiar and far more congenial.

In later years her daughter, Hannie, detailed how difficult it was for her mother to adjust to living in a culture so different from the one she was formed in. The food, rhythms of life, and climate always remained alien to her. There is no record of how well she spoke Bahasa, the language of the region. Theodora seems to have constructed her own alternative pattern of life, if not reality, when she lived in the East Indies, right down to preparing Dutch food daily for herself. It must also have been difficult for her as a young Western woman, perhaps pampered at home, not to have the full attention of her energetic and capable husband who increasingly became involved in his work as he advanced in his ability to manage. Hannie could state forthrightly that her parents had a difficult relationship because of these factors. Whether from personal character or conformity, however, there never was a hint or suggestion that they ever thought of separating or dissolving their marriage. The return to The Hague with the birth of a little boy during this stay suggests that the leave literally breathed new life into their relationship, at least for a while.

By 1924 H.R. Rookmaaker, Senior was back in the Dutch Indies with his family. He now served as the Controller of a colonial administrative division in the middle of the western part of Sumatra. One imagines that Hans Rookmaaker's first sense of his own personal identity must have occurred around this time, physically and geographically faraway from where he was born, on the way to or in a land that was in many ways the polar opposite of the land of his adult years.

Photos of the three- or four-year-old Hans Rookmaaker suggest he was a handful. He is a bundle of energy with a closely shaven head of hair and a barrel of monkeyshines just waiting to be let loose. In one small but revealing picture his older sister, Door, is obviously trying to hold him still for a serious family photograph, while he is totally distracted and attempting to break away from her. It is a telling family portrait. Father Henderik faces the camera intently and frontally, uniformed properly as a colonial official with his pith helmet in his hand at his side. One can almost feel the equatorial heat and glare of the sun in his eyes as he tries to focus them straight at the camera. Mother, Theodora, stands firmly at his side, visibly a much stouter woman than she was a decade earlier. She strains her eyes toward the camera without any evidence of regard for her eldest daughter at her side trying her best to keep little Hans (Hansje) literally in the picture. Hannie, the younger daughter, stands before her parents most respectfully, one hand clasping the other. Her face is bowed in shadow. One wonders whether her posture was because of the bright sun shining above or because she was feeling awkward and embarrassed to be part of this kind of family photo. Perhaps it was both.

Door, ten years older than her brother, became very much his little mother. Other family photos show her keeping an eye on him, holding his hand or standing behind him literally and figuratively. Though she married, she herself never had children of her own. She would outlive her brother by more than a decade, showing concern toward the end of her life for his children.

There seem to be more photos of Hans as a child with his father than with his mother. In a photo taken of him with his mother in The Hague at the age of ten, he stands by her side, leaning toward her slightly with a clear expression of apprehension and real anxiety on his face. She faces the camera squarely and resolutely, without even a trace of a smile on her face.

As the baby of the family, Hans was spoiled to a certain degree. Servants abounded in his colonial home to meet his physical requirements more than amply. If his mother was not overly attentive, his sisters adored him. His father, though reserved and not especially demonstrative, clearly took an interest in his son and was proud of him as a boy and as a young man. Hans in turn was proud of his father. Throughout his life he often expressed his admiration for the Resident. His father was in many ways a remarkable man. Even by today's standards he can be considered a rather enlightened colonial official. Hans absorbed many of his father's qualities. In his adult years this can be seen in his personal discipline and professional diligence, his willingness to take on responsibility, his eagerness to learn not inconsiderable organizational skill, and his great love for the beauty of nature.

During his career as a colonial official, H.R. Rookmaaker, Senior was recognized for his outstanding abilities. The peak of his career was when he was promoted to become Resident of the Lampong districts of southern Sumatra. There he was active not only in organizing but taking the leadership in persuading and motivating people from the more populous Java to immigrate to the southern part of Sumatra to develop parts of it barely thought to be habitable. He did not lure migrants under false pretenses. He said it would be difficult for them, they would need to sacrifice, and they would need to pay with hard labor before they received any benefit from their move. In short, it proved to be a successful experiment of indigenous people colonizing another part of the region voluntarily. For this achievement he received the Oranje-Nassau medal from his government.

Before his final departure from his post in Sumatra, Rookmaaker, Senior also initiated the protection of the forests. Through his efforts the South Sumatra and Way Kambas National Parks were formed. He tried to convince his colonial colleagues that elephants and other animals needed protected areas to live in so they would be preserved from attack. All of this was quite extraordinary at a time when the idea that it was important to safeguard nature from increasing human incursion was rarely discussed by fellow government officials.

The active interest that Hans's father took in plants and animals created a conscious awareness and appreciation of rare creatures right at home. A young boy might be expected to find the business of his father boring, but a boy could not be indifferent to a father bringing home with him live birds and other kinds of exotic wild animals, many of which had been injured. There is an old snapshot of Rookmaaker, Senior dressed in a white suit sitting at a table with an exquisite floral arrangement in a classically colonial setting holding a little rodent-like creature on his arm. His entire concentration is focused on this small furry animal with a long tail as he strokes it ever so gently.

By 1927 Hans's father had become a serious naturalist who loved to explore the rich and complex world of natural phenomena around him. He frequently took his children with him on his explorations. Although Hans was probably too young to accompany his father on his expedition to capture Komodo dragons in 1927, it must have brought an enormous amount of excitement into his home as it was discussed, and these largest of the earth's monitor-type lizards in transit perhaps were viewed by the boy. Systematic scientific study of these giant monitors was just beginning. In total, twelve Komodo dragons were captured and sent to zoological gardens and centers of study in Europe. As these ferocious primordial-looking beasts are huge, on average around eight feet long, and have long, forked yellow tongues that can lash out to more than a foot, it must have been no small undertaking to capture them. Thereafter two newly identified species were named after Rookmaaker, Senior: the frog *Oreophryne rookmaakeri* (1927) and the shell *Xesta rookmaakeri* (1930). One of the birds he collected was later (1948) identified as a new subspecies and named for him—*Mesia argentauris rookmakeri* (spelling his name incorrectly).

In 1929 Rookmaaker, Senior was an Assistant-Resident based at Lho Semaweh (Lhokseumawe) on the north coast of Aceh in Sumatra. Part of his official duties had always been to entertain visiting dignitaries. In that year, when Hans was seven years old, his father welcomed Prince Leopold of Belgium (1901–1983) to Lho Semaweh and hosted various events for him, including a rather sumptuous banquet. Five years later the Prince was to become King Leopold III of Belgium. The Belgian professor Victor Van Straelen (1889–1964) accompanied the twenty-eight-year-old prince. Van Straelen was a noted international naturalist, pioneering conservation and parks in Central Africa as well as in the Galpagos Islands. Family photos and reminiscences emphasize the royal visitor, but the professor's visit may well have had a more lasting impact on and been a formative factor for Rookmaaker's own education regarding natural preservation that he pioneered later in southern Sumatra. For his hospitality and helpfulness in showing the prince and professor around the natural wonders of this part of the world, Hans's father received a Belgian medal of appreciation.

In 1931 the Rookmaaker family returned to the Netherlands on a year's leave. Once again they lived in The Hague. Hans was nine years old. By this time he'd had more moves in his life than most people even in present-day mobile Western culture have in a lifetime. His sisters were in their late teens; he was not yet an adolescent. His education through travel and meeting an unusually wide spectrum of people must have outstripped his formal schooling. Hans was a resilient child who learned well despite a constant stream of changing schools and new teachers on two different continents. Intellectually he was ahead of his age. When his family returned to the Dutch Indies, an experiment of placing him in a class ahead of his age and sending him to boarding school in another part of the island group proved unsuccessful. He may not have had a perfect family, but apparently he appreciated being near them and was a better learner as a result of this security amidst a sea of constant change.

H.R. Rookmaaker, Senior's Residency in Sumatra was cut short by ill health. In 1936 he returned to the Netherlands to live in The Hague. The official termination of his Residency occurred in 1937. He may have tried to return to his post briefly, but a heart condition finally forced him into retirement. The Rookmaakers lived through the war years in The Hague.

With his father's help and counsel, Hans opted to make an important educational choice. Instead of going to a secondary school for a classical education with Latin and Greek, he chose the five-year course of a technical high school in Leiden. With constant moving about, life had never been exactly convenient for Hans. Now the uncertainty of his parents' future in regard to his father's health and professional life left the family at loose ends concerning their son's schooling. Finally a difficult decision was made for Hans—to live temporarily with relatives in Leiden while he went to school there.

Hans's high school education next led him to Den Helder, the famous Dutch naval college located at the far northwestern tip of the Netherlands, where the best and brightest were enrolled to be apprenticed to serve the future of their country.

Meanwhile, somewhere along the way this emerging youth fell in love with African-American music and opened himself to it. He began to amass a collection of records of the blues, jazz, and spirituals that in his adulthood would become one of the most important sources in Europe for this kind of music. There is no evidence that he was a particularly rebellious youth asserting himself by taking up this type of music, though in later years he personally exhibited great empathy for youth who were full of protest and who gravitated to styles of music that were guaranteed to offend the bourgeois sensibilities of their parents.

Music and dance were in the air of this era. On both sides of the Atlantic and beyond, young people and not so young people kicked up their heels and danced, desiring to become celebrative after the economically lean years of the 1920s in the wake of World War I. A marvelous snapshot of Rookmaaker, Senior from the 1930s shows him playfully and exuberantly bursting out with an *oleé* or a flamenco or going along for a real run at a rumba. His son joyously followed in his father's footsteps when it came to enjoying this kind of fun.

Constant change, cultural complexities, and emotional ambiguities filled Hans Rookmaaker's childhood. He experienced many privileges. He also experienced many uncertainties. Instead of being demoralized by these conditions, he seems to have allowed them to shape his self-confidence, shielding him from a feeling of being too much of an outsider or stranger. As the days ahead would show, this capable and in many ways self-assured child still sought a true home for heart and head and hand to dwell in.

THREE

YOUTH

Hans Rookmaaker grew up as a secular young person. It is difficult to tell whether attending a Christian Reformed high school influenced him at all. As a well-meaning official and parent, Rookmaaker, Senior, definitely not a pious person, told his children emphatically and even profanely that they should attend church on important occasions whether they felt like it or not!

Hans's religious sensibilities would wait to be developed. He described his own religious upbringing in this way:

I come from a family that can in no way be described as religious. There was no profound opposition to religion. My father did believe that God existed and that the Bible was a worthwhile book—perhaps his grandparents had been Protestants—but that was all. They even forgot to have me baptized. As a boy I did go to a Christian secondary school—because it was such a good one—but I was not in any way reached by the gospel there. It is really remarkable, by the way, how little mission-minded Dutch Christians often are. Apart from one conversation with one of my teachers no one ever tried to tell me anything more of the gospel. (CW, 2:10)

By the late 1930s when Hans was in his formative teenage years, the world of the Dutch Indies was behind him. The Dutch colonial enterprise was crumbling, and a new nation, Indonesia, was slowly coming into existence despite an added struggle of resistance through three years of Japanese occupation during World War II. Hans's father had been one of the last and best colonial administrators, but the paternalistic world he served and the need for men like him were disappearing. No longer able to discharge his duties due to illness, and after a brief stint in the Ministry of Finance, Hans's father ailed on in The Hague on government disability allowance, no doubt astutely observing these changes abroad and perhaps even glad he did not have to deal with them directly. Hans's mother resumed a social life that suited her far more than that in the Dutch Indies.

The young Rookmaaker's interests burgeoned. Intellectually, he did as well at mathematics and science as he did at history and the humanities. He had a special interest in ship design. One supposes his fascination with ships developed in the weeks he had spent since childhood sailing to and from the Netherlands and around the Spice Islands. Based on these interests and the changing situation overseas, a career in the navy probably looked a lot more promising than any consideration of following in the Rookmaaker tradition of colonial civil service.

Hans's real passion, however, was for music, especially authentic African-American music. He was not interested in the modified styles created to cater to a consumerist white audience.

From the beginning he demanded the genuine thing. He listened over and over to the same pieces. Precociously he developed a discerning taste for the nuances of this music and a considerable knowledge of its development. He also became an almost obsessive record collector. He spent any available money he had on records and regularly borrowed them from or traded them with his friends.

Physically he was filling out from a somewhat scrawny child to his adult height of five feet, eight inches. A high school photo shows the face of a serious but pleasant-looking young man with dark brown hair and eyes. In somewhat later pictures of him in his naval cadet's uniform he even looks rather dashing.

Although the Dutch navy had officially been in existence since 1488, the Royal Netherlands Naval College at Den Helder was not established until the middle of the nineteenth century. As Den Helder was an important naval base and shipyard, it was decided that this would be an ideal location for educating midshipmen. Its first official classrooms were built on the grounds of the state shipyard. In 1854 it opened with twenty-five cadets enrolled. In 1939, the last year Hans Rookmaaker was a midshipman (*adelborst*) there and on the eve of the college's closure in 1940 by the Germans, there were ninety-eight naval cadets. It was a select group with its own special traditions. Interestingly, many of the midshipmen at Den Helder managed to escape to England when the German occupation of the Netherlands occurred. There they continued their naval training at a base in Cornwall. A naval institute was also organized at Surabaya in the Dutch East Indies, but it was forced to close in 1942 at the time of the Japanese invasion.

One wonders whether Hans Rookmaaker had a chance to choose to escape in 1940 as some of his fellow midshipmen did. By that time there were compelling factors in his life to keep him close to home and prevent him from running away, even if he'd had the opportunity or felt convinced he could have helped the war effort by being outside the country. Although his sister Door by this time had married and was living with her husband in the Dutch Indies, in The Hague he still had a single sister and parents with health problems who concerned him and needed him. But even beyond these important reasons was a factor of far greater significance for the course of his life. Hans Rookmaaker was deeply in love and, though young, had become engaged.

Sometime during those naval cadet years, Hans, who not only loved music but also loved to dance, for want of a date invited or perhaps dragged along his older sister, Hannie, to go out dancing with him one evening when he was at home. Not long after their arrival at the dance club, Hannie recognized an acquaintance of hers across the room.

Hannie liked to take complete credit for introducing her brother to her friend, Riki Spetter, that evening. She also declared it was love at first sight for both of them.

They both met what they thought was their match. Hendrika Beatrix (nicknamed Riki) Spetter was born on May 10, 1919 into a middle-class Jewish family who lived in The Hague. She was one of five children. She had an older sister and three brothers. She was three years older than Hans, but this difference of age, usually so discernible in teenage years, was probably not too noticeable. By this time Hans was adept at relating to older young ladies. His sisters were respectively ten and eight years older than he was, and they gave him ample observation of their ways as well as tutelage in how to make an impression on what in those days was considered the fairer sex.

From photos, personal accounts, and her loving letters to Hans while he was in prison, first at Scheveningen near The Hague and later at Langwasser near Nuremberg, we can gain a glimpse of this young woman. Her life was to be tragically brief. She and her entire family, save for her brother, Max, who was in the Dutch East Indies at the time, were swept away by the Nazis.

She was a special person. Although Hans was barely eighteen years old, their relationship was not a case of an ignorant, youthful infatuation. Hans was genuinely a mature young man for his age. Riki had some inspiring qualities. Anky Huitker, her friend and clerical office colleague, who later became Hans's wife, knew her and her family well and always maintained an admiration and respect coupled with affection for her.

Riki had sparkle. She was not conventionally beautiful at all but was attractive and exuded personality. Her hair was not quite brown but a dark blonde. This we know, for she touchingly attached a lock of it to one of her last letters to Hans. Photos of her rival that of Hans's father doing the rumba. One snapshot shows her holding a perky cat on her shoulder, her arm raised high above her head with some tasty little bit in her hand that the feline is totally transfixed on and ready to devour. She expresses total absorption and joy in this creature's anticipation of attacking its prey. Another snapshot shows her playfully taking a draw on Hans's pipe as she languidly lounges on a daybed. Another picture shows a solemn and domestic side to her. Sitting before the same daybed with batik hangings behind it, slim and serious, she looks intently into the camera as she knits. Her face suggests a certain realistic awareness of life.

Despite the ominous situation of a war on their doorstep, Hans and Riki enjoyed some months of joy and enjoyment in each other's company. They were a convivial couple. There was much coming and going between their homes and their friends' homes. They delighted in listening to music and dancing and talking half the night away—a habit that Hans never grew out of or gave up, if given a chance. But new love and romance would not last long for either of them.

When Den Helder was closed after the Nazi occupation that took place on May 10, 1940 at Whitsuntide (also the date of Riki's birthday), Hans, still technically a commissioned officer in the Dutch navy (sergeant—*adelborst*), transferred to a course in engineering at Delft Technical University. This was much nearer his family and his fiancée, all of whom continued to live in The Hague. Despite occupation there was still some regularity in the daily pattern of his life until March 4, 1941. On that day he was arrested for possession of *deutschfeindliche Flugschriften* ("anti-German literature").

It came about that one of his lecturers at the university, René Donker, had passed on to him a pamphlet entitled *De vrije Katheder* ("The Free Podium"). He had been caught with this in his pocket. Along with Donker and two other defendants, he had to stand trial nine months later in December 1941. He was the youngest of the four of them. He seems to have been in custody the entire time from March to December 1941. That meant missing the best part of an academic year. Although it is ambiguous, it seems that the two and a half months he was sentenced to for his "crime" was assigned retroactively. Nevertheless, he still had spent six and a half months in jail, as it seemed, for nothing.

During that time Riki and his family worried about him greatly every day. Mostly his father, Hannie, and Riki wrote loving communal letters to him, asking what they could do or send to him. He was allowed to write notes and letters to his family. And they were able to answer and send him some essentials of survival, such as his toothbrush, extra blankets, and books. It must have been both hard and odd to have him incarcerated in the maximum security prison of Scheveningen, right on their doorstep in The Hague, without being able to see or visit him.

At this point, time was a lot more precious than any of them probably realized. After Hans's release from Scheveningen Prison there were to be only five months before commissioned officers like him were commanded by the Nazis to report in Breda, a city historically associated with the Royal Netherlands Military Academy. That call came in April 1942. From this center, Rookmaaker was dispatched with a group that became Oflag 67 (*Offizierslager für kriegsgefangene Offiziere* = "POW camp for officers 67"). They were sent to Langwasser in the southeast environs of Nuremberg in Bavaria.

From the time that Hans had returned from the Dutch East Indies to the Netherlands in 1936, his life had begun unfolding at a rapid rate. He was forced to grow up quickly. He had to make difficult decisions about his education. He had to deal with dramatic experiences in his life that he chose to embrace and ones that he had no control over whatsoever. The gravity of life and his own serious nature were beginning to open him to the realities of a spiritual and religious dimension to his life that he never had fully acknowledged or engaged before. The days ahead would change him and the conditions of his life forever.

In the meantime Riki kept up a courageous spirit. She had remained constant in her loyalty to him while he was in Scheveningen Prison. She had written to him consistently, and did the same when he was being held in Germany. Her letters were filled with endearing sweetness, but without sentimentality. At the same time she also took on a major amount of responsibility in caring for her sick mother. She tried to enjoy herself and reported to Hans about going here and there, to this one's and that one's house to talk and listen to music. She tried to hunt down special rare records and books that he was looking for. In a July 6, 1942 letter she wrote:

> My dearest,
> The book *From Socrates to Bergson* that you wanted me to get for you is not available any more . . . [regarding] records I was in the shops, but no good ones are coming out. I am anxious to hear from you. How often can you write? I walk to the mailbox every day, but there is nothing from you. Patience is supposed to be such a beautiful thing, but I don't see much in it.
>
> Your always loving,
> Riki

Gradually the Nazi regime was becoming more and more of a daily repressive reality for Jews in the Netherlands. Public transport was not available for Jews, and Riki had to walk everywhere, including to her work. Negotiating the everyday necessities of shopping meant that daily errands took doubly long. It became a major undertaking to go over to the Rookmaakers' home and discuss with them Hans's situation and the news of the day or to sit down all together to write a letter to him.

More and more social events happened at her own parental home. Her friends thought that coming to her home would be more convenient than her having to walk a long way or alone to their homes. Although she was a welcoming and hospitable person and she seemed to have had an open family, it became a burden to always have to be the host, no matter how well meaning her friends' intentions were for her benefit.

The last letters that she wrote to Hans were positive, even as she faced the unthinkable and the unimaginable. Her spirit never wavered. Her maturity was exemplary. She also showed herself to be spiritually-minded. On August 10, 1942 she wrote to Hans: "I am reading a lot in the Bible, but [there is] much that I don't understand and you must explain it when you return." There is also evidence in her letters that she was beginning to pray.

By the end of the third week of August 1942, Riki's family, except for one brother who at that time was in the Dutch East Indies, was taken from The Hague and sent to a detention center in Westerbork in the Drenthe province in the northern part of the country, midway between Zwolle and Groningen. Afterward they were transported to Auschwitz, where they were killed by the Nazis.

When Riki could no longer write, her friend Anky Huitker, whose family courageously hid Jewish people in their home during the war, sadly informed Hans of what had taken place. Apparently Hans had written to Anky beforehand to ask her to buy some flowers for Riki as a favor for him. Anky wrote:

Dear Hans,
Finally, I'll answer your postcard. I was glad to hear from you.
I took care of the flowers, and she was very happy. . . .

[But the] news now is very sad. Riki . . . with her whole family was moved on 18 August to Drenthe (Assen). Riki felt terrible to leave The Hague, but [it was] a big comfort that they all went together. She kept up her courage [and] put on a brave face. I have to say she probably can't write to you, but she will think of you all the time. If ever [it is] possible, she will write. I really admire Riki in the last weeks—how she handled all this difficulty. She was the strongest of the family.

Riki asked at the last moment that I should write that you should not be anxious because she feels she has inner fortitude. She was unbelievably competent.

As soon as I hear from her, I will let you know. But, [I think] it will be long, because they cannot write to us. . . .

Many kind greetings from all here who know you,
Anky

The monstrous insanity and oppression of Nazi ideology and war wiped out this promising young life, as it did so many other innocent lives. Only gradually did Hans come to understand and realize the magnitude of his personal loss. Hans's sisters felt that at some level he probably never recovered from the crushing blow of losing Riki. It was a double loss, for at the same time he experienced the premature loss of his own youth.

FOUR

CONVERSION AND CALLING

Almost the first thing Hans Rookmaaker did when he returned after the war to the Netherlands was to place advertisements in newspapers in several Dutch cities asking if anyone had seen or had any knowledge of Riki Spetter, who had been seen last at Westerbork on August 18, 1942. Although what Anky Huitker had written to him regarding Riki's being taken away by the German occupiers had not reassured him that he would hear from her, it had understandably left the door open for some hope. It was a hope that Hans carried with him through the rest of the war years.

Riki's last letter to Hans was addressed to him at a field post address (Feldpostadresse 45667). This was a different address from the one she had been writing to at Nuremberg-Langwasser just six days earlier, on August 4, 1942.

Shortly after Hans's call in April 1942 to report with other commissioned officers to Breda, he was transported with a group of his fellow officers to the very center of the fanatical Führer cult at Nuremberg. It was here that the infamous Nazi Party Rally Grounds, designed in 1934 by Hitler's favorite architect Albert Speer, were located. A camp zone southeast and adjacent to the Party Rally Grounds from 1939 on served as a prisoner-of-war camp. This was Langwasser (today a suburb of Nuremberg), where Oflag 67, Rookmaaker's designated camp, was located.

Up until 1943 inmates at this camp labored for the city of Nuremberg on the construction of the Party Rally Grounds. Hans probably spent most of the summer there. After breaking its nonaggression pact with the Soviet Union by invading its vast territory in June 1941, Germany was almost completely strapped for a workforce. Every able-bodied person was serving in the armed forces in an insane war that was being battled on several fronts. Whether serving major industry or pet projects of the Führer, forced foreign labor had become part of Nazi party policy.

From the change of address on Riki's letter to Hans on August 10, 1942, it seems she must have heard from him that he was being moved from Nuremberg-Langwasser. Over a month later Hans began sending letters to his family from a camp unit that was designated Stalag 371. It was situated in Stanislau in the historic region known as Galicia, an area that is part of western Ukraine. Although considered a territory of Poland from 1919 to 1939, this place was part of the German-occupied Soviet Union when Hans was there. Today this city, nestling amidst the northeastern foothills of the Carpathian Mountains, is known as Ivano Frankivsk. Until 1962 it was called Stanislau, when it was renamed to honor the Ukrainian poet Ivan Franko (1856–1916). Many, if not most, of the prisoners of Stalag 371 were Dutch.

From an incident that took place on June 4, 1943 in Saxony at Colditz Castle, a notorious, maximum-security prison reserved for elite foreign prisoners, we know of an attempted escape by Dutch inmates that linked them to Stalag 371. They chose that date because they knew they were soon going to be moved to Stanislau. The link between Colditz Castle and Stanislau and the Dutch is interesting. Hans may have stayed there temporarily on his way to Stanislau when Riki sent him the letter addressed to a German field post.

At any rate, by June 1943 when the Dutch contingency from Colditz Castle arrived in Stanislau, Hans already had been there nine months. He was to stay there until sometime in February 1944. In the seventeen or eighteen months that Hans was at Stanislau, a profound transformation that had begun in Nuremberg, or even earlier, took place in his life.

Reading between the lines of Riki's letters, it appears that Hans started a serious reading and consideration of the Bible. In an essay published in 1967 he wrote that he had started thinking seriously about spiritual matters

> . . . after the German invasion of the Netherlands in May 1940. I then went to study in Delft, to await the end of the war. In those days I began to think more seriously about matters, and sometimes I had the feeling that God could play an important role in our lives. But only when I, along with other professional officers, was made a prisoner of war and landed in a camp near Nuremberg did I begin to think about seriously reading the Bible. There were no other books available and, as a civilized man with cultural interests, I thought it would be good to know something about it. As I was reading, I gradually came to the conviction that the Bible reveals the truth to us. (CW, 2:10)

The relatively long stay of over a year at Stanislau allowed Rookmaaker more time for sustained thought and reflection.

> I spent a lot of time thinking about the Christian faith, but read very little about it. Apart from this I made good use of the

time. Gradually, especially after our POW camp was moved to Stanislau, more books became available. One man had this book and the next, another. I read philosophy, psychology, literature and especially the history of literature; in short, from all sorts of fields in the humanities. I also continued to work clandestinely to finish my training as naval officer while we officially had the opportunity to continue studying through Delft University; I even sat exams. I did all the mathematical subjects. (CW, 2:10)

Gradually the young officer and diligent student was going beyond merely educating himself in order to become a more cultured person to making a definite decision about the future course of his thinking and, indeed, about who he personally was becoming. At Stanislau he apprenticed himself to mastering the Bible. The curious, abridged version of the Dutch Bible that he had at his disposal during this time is marked and cross-referenced in a range of handwritings that suggests the wide range of his emotions during these months. It reflects a mind that remembered the content of the Testaments, Old and New, as they related to each other and made an impact on him. It shows an ardency and intense engagement in a personal way with the Scripture that continued to be borne out all through his life.

The very first lines to be underlined in this Bible deal not with a possibly abstract doctrine of the nature of man that might be expected to be derived by an intellectual from Genesis 1:27, but with a text that would have been existential for him then in regard to his desire to be married. It is the text, "Therefore a man leaves his father and his mother and clings to his wife, and they become one flesh" (Genesis 2:24, *New Revised Standard Version*). Cross-referenced with this is Paul's great exhortation in Ephesians 5:25–33 for husbands to love their wives just as Christ loved the church and gave himself up for her.

Rookmaaker read the Bible in a personally participative

way. This did not mean he read it subjectively. He faced hard and difficult passages and let them judge him. In a sense he let the Scripture read his life as much as he read the sacred text.

While still a prisoner of war he wrote two documents that in many ways presciently foreshadowed the task and mission of the rest of his life. "Prophecy in the Old and New Testaments" (*"Betreffende de Profetie"*) is the first. *"Aesthetica"* is the second. Both are carefully written in the hand of someone who knows how precious a piece of paper is when you do not know where the next scrap might come from. Not a space is wasted in these student-like composition books of approximately eighty pages.

On September 19, 1943, Rookmaaker movingly dedicated his study of the Old Testament prophets to Riki. In it he explores his reading of Scripture in order to understand how the Old Testament/Hebrew Bible is related to and fulfilled in the New Testament and how prophetic utterances might have contemporary meaning. This endeavor seems to have undergirded his other studies on a wide range of subjects during his time at Stanislau. Other than *"Aesthetica,"* begun almost two years later, it appears to be the only record of systematic studies made while a POW that he endeavored to preserve and brought back with him to the Netherlands after the war. Toward the end of his time at Stanislau, Hans came into contact with a person who proved to be one of the most influential and faithful friends of his life. The relationship almost certainly did not start on a peer basis. Johan Pieter Albertus (J.P.A.) Mekkes (1897–1987) was twenty-five years older than Rookmaaker. Mekkes was a convinced Christian and a deeply intellectual man. He was a professional army man and ranked as a captain in the ground forces. At exactly the right time, Mekkes appeared as a mature and willing guide for this self-taught beginner.

As Hans did not seem to be aware of his presence at Stanislau before the second half of 1943, it may have been that Mekkes came to Stalag 371 with the elite Dutch group that arrived some time in the summer of that year from Castle Colditz in Germany. They both were not to remain at Stanislau for much longer, for the Soviets were starting to push the Germans back on the eastern front. At the end of 1943 or possibly at the very beginning of 1944, Stalag 371 was evacuated to Neubrandenburg, a city north of Berlin and about halfway to the Baltic in Mecklenburg-Lower Pomerania. Hans's correspondence confirms he was in Germany by February 24, 1944. Meanwhile, Mekkes and Rookmaaker wasted no time in becoming acquainted.

To attain the rank of captain, Mekkes must have had exceptional leadership qualities and the ability to develop and educate younger men. A photo of him when he was probably in his sixties suggests he was an urbane man. His letters to Hans show a man of great warmth and character. Mekkes, too, was a self-learner. He started his doctoral studies in philosophical law even while he was in the army. He must have naturally admired Hans when he saw how eagerly this young officer desired to learn. It must have also intrigued him that Hans was inclined to study both Scripture and philosophy, precisely his own interests. Hans in turn knew that here was someone who could help him. Here was a mentor who could cultivate his interests and talents to new and higher levels as well as confirm his growing conviction of the truth of the Bible and the Christian faith.

Rookmaaker told of meeting Mekkes in his essay, "What the Philosophy of the Cosmonomic Idea Has Meant to Me":

> During that decisive time, I was introduced to Captain (later Professor) Mekkes. It was just at the time that we were being evacuated to Neubrandenburg. I heard about Dooyeweerd from Captain Mekkes and started to read Dooyeweerd's book [De Wijsbegeerte der Wetsidee, 1935–1936]. Rather, I devoured it. For I discovered, right from page 1, that someone was speaking who started with precisely this question [of whether there would be a place for philosophy within Christian belief], and offered a clear solution, namely that

"modal law-spheres" was a ready-made formula for a rigid form of Fundamentalism. It is not that this cannot happen (Rookmaaker learned soon enough about the rigidly Reformed), but it would be a serious mistake to say that this combination had that effect on him. With his own words he states that what he found Dooyeweerd saying was, "the Christian's thinking is not closed off, but is actually opened up." In a striking way he discovered for himself a classical Christian formulation of Anselm following Augustine: *credo ut intelligam* ("I believe in order that I may understand"). Something dynamic and clarifying had happened to his thinking that he was convinced gave his ideas a firm intellectual foundation while allowing them to roam and range and soar over the whole wide world.

During the darkest days of the war, Hans Rookmaaker experienced the light of new life in Christ. While physically confined and captive in Germany, he became spiritually and intellectually liberated. Amazingly his conversion translated almost seamlessly into a calling for his life's work and mission. A new assurance of identity, however, did not automatically transfer into a crystal-clear idea of a career path or the formation of a family based on a reunion with a much loved fiancée. He still had an arduous apprenticeship before him to find his way professionally and to grow into a maturity upon which a marriage could be built.

FIVE

FAMILY AND CAREER

Weaving the strands of life together again after the war was not simple. These years were active, full, and complex ones for Hans.

He knew for almost the entire time of his imprisonment that Riki Spetter, his Jewish fiancée, had been taken away with her family from The Hague to the province of Drenthe in the north of Holland. Nevertheless, he continued to hope and to write letters to Riki via his family during all that time. Only in January 1945 did he admit how "sad that we cannot write letters to Riki anymore, but understandable."

Prior to this he was full of hope. His longing was palpable.

He shared the whole gamut of his life with her, despite not knowing whether she would ever even see his letters.

> O, Riki, when will we be together again to talk, to talk about things that are so dear to our hearts and about what you cannot say and express so easily in a letter? I hope you still read the Bible regularly and that you still have peace and trust in God. I pray always that He will give you His grace so that you can have faith in Him. [April 2, 1944]

> My dearest Riki, I just listened to my record of the violin concerto of Beethoven. How wonderful now and then to enjoy music. Later, we will listen together to concerts and records. A cat has just given birth to kittens in the barracks. We are taking care of the mother. The kittens, of course, [are being taken care of] by the mother. . . . I am lately occupied with a Christian philosophy. . . . Later, I will explain it to you when we can talk again. Luckily, there is someone here in the camp who has studied this philosophy and can give guidance in this subject. I always hope you can find peace and trust in God. I am so happy that we talked about this the last day we were together. I hope it is still like that with you. [April 22, 1944]

> Dearest Riki, . . . There will be an end to this war. We will come together again. . . . I hope and always pray that you can endure and find that God may give you faith from which you can draw strength and power. [December 27, 1944]

The Russian offensive had continued to push westward since the time Rookmaaker and Mekkes and their fellow prisoners were hastily evacuated from Stanislau in the western Ukraine to the overcrowded POW camp at Neubrandenburg about sixty miles north of Berlin. By mid-January 1945 the Russians had swept into Poland, occupied Warsaw, and were pressing on to Germany's East Prussian frontier. In March and early April the Germans marched some groups of prisoners from

Neubrandenburg west toward the Elbe and others north toward Rostock. Apparently Hans was one of those who remained until ragtag Russian soldiers, probably the Army of the Belorussian Front, occupied the poorly supplied camp on April 28, 1945 and theoretically liberated it. But there were still problems. The Red Army harassed some of the ailing prisoners, and there was some indentured service for a time as the occupation of the surrounding area was secured. Food and medical shortages were acute. Eventually (it is not clear how) Hans made it home to The Hague after the European armistice of May 8, 1945. The Netherlands had been liberated prior to this on May 5.

The last part of his captivity probably was the worst in terms of physical deprivation. His letters from Stanislau and Neubrandenburg reveal a surprising amount of abundance for wartime. Before leaving Stanislau he sent a suitcase filled with tobacco, chocolate, and other foodstuffs to his family in the Netherlands. He felt they needed it more than he did! Camp authorities ordered the inmates to get rid of anything they were not prepared to carry. Hans decided he would be glad to carry his winter coat with him. These luxury items that he packed in his suitcase to send home seem to have been sent by the Red Cross or some other international charitable agency. During his time in the POW camp, he received food and various items from a number of places in the world, including Argentina and America. While he was at Neubrandenburg he also had his family send him some of his favorite jazz records.

Rookmaaker acquired an amazing education while in the POW camp. He worked on a wide range of the humanities, including the Greek and Latin he had missed by not attending a classically oriented secondary school. He also studied technical subjects. He had his family send him all sorts of specialized books pertaining to the type of studies he had been doing at Delft Technical University. He even officially sat for exams in mathematics and other scientific subjects. Clandestinely he also pursued his training as a naval officer. And, of course, there was his intensive study of Scripture and the Christian philosophy known as the Philosophy of the Cosmonomic Idea, pioneered by Herman Dooyeweerd.

Riki had written to Hans, "I am reading a lot in the Bible, but [there is] much that I don't understand and you must explain it when you return." There seems little doubt that this sober plea and his love for her propelled the serious and systematic study of the Hebrew prophets and God's way with Israel that he started at Stanislau. She inspired the beginning of his investigation, and he dedicated it to her. She was also present at the conclusion. At the center of the back cover of the notebook he used, he drew two capital R's, for Riki and Rookmaaker, that he symmetrically linked with a crossbar, forming a visual double entendre for HRR.

On Hans's return to The Hague and even before trying to find Riki, he had to address the dramatically changed circumstances of his own immediate family and his country. The armistice with Germany was just two days short of exactly five years of German occupation of the Netherlands that had begun on May 10, 1940. He had spent most of those years in detention, first for nine months at Scheveningen Prison near The Hague and afterward slightly over three years in at least three different German POW camps. His brother-in-law, Gerard Rotgans, who managed to be abroad during the war, had written to him at Neubrandenburg to say that he could "barely imagine how Holland look[ed]." During the last months and days of the war, life in Holland was extremely grim, especially with shortages of food, fuel, and medical supplies.

The first grave reality that Hans had to face was that his father had died in his absence. The war years had taken a terrible toll on the former colonial official. Eleven days before Rookmaaker, Senior's death on January 31, 1945, Hans had written from Neubrandenburg:

> It is freezing here all the time in these last months, but luckily not too much because the heating here is so-so. How is every-

one's health? I hope you can get through all the difficulties. . . . I hope the food parcels will arrive soon. . . . I am very glad you received the last package I sent to Holland. Now I hope everything finishes soon. [January 20, 1945]

Sadly, Hans's father did not live to see his son return home, nor the defeat of Germany and the end of its brutal occupation of his country. His health had been compromised from the late 1930s when he was forced into an early retirement after a couple of attempts to resume his career. The war only undermined his health all the more. For unknown reasons the Rookmaakers had to move to another house in The Hague during wartime. They also experienced hunger and cold. Apparently after the strenuous activity of chopping firewood, Rookmaaker (Pappie) died of a heart attack at the age of fifty-seven.

Hans's mother (Mammie) was fifty-five years old when he returned. She was a sorrowing widow and had lost the pillar of her security and the compass of her family life. Physically she showed stamina and survived the war years relatively well, but mentally she exhibited signs that she was not fully emotionally stable. It was inevitable that she would look to her son for support and make demands, perhaps not totally consciously, on him. By this time both of his sisters, Door and Hannie, were married. This alleviated the pressures of his being the only responsible adult male in the family. His siblings and their spouses, however, were scattered. Door and her husband, Dick Haver Droeze, had spent the war in the Japanese-occupied Dutch Indies. Armistice there did not come until later, at the beginning of September 1945, nearly three months after it had been declared in Europe. Hannie's husband, Gerard, was abroad. All of this meant that a great deal of responsibility was still placed on the shoulders of a young man of twenty-three.

The big question loomed over him: Where was Riki? He placed advertisements in the newspapers in The Hague, Amsterdam, Utrecht, and Leeuwarden to see if anyone had been in contact with her or knew of her whereabouts since she was last seen in Westerbork in August 1942. He must have felt increasingly crushed as no response to his campaign to find her materialized, including asking the old network of mutual friends who remained from pre-war days.

The changed external circumstances of his country and his family and personal life perhaps were not the most drastic challenges Hans faced on his return home. He had changed radically, more profoundly than he himself may have been aware of at the time. It was a shock to his family, especially his adoring sisters, to find that their beloved brother had returned filled with religion and talk of Christian philosophy. They knew their Hans was clever and loved to study. They knew he had found solace in his studies during his detention. But they were not prepared for the fact that a significant part of his passion for learning had led him to a vigorous faith informing everything he thought about and wanted to do with his life. As his family had no particular religious heritage, his fervency seemed to them like fanaticism. In the following years shock transmuted to anger. Hannie and her husband, Gerard, tried to reason Hans out of his stance. Until her last days Hannie showed considerable resistance and hostility to her brother's beliefs.

Meanwhile, he was acquiring a new spiritual family that expanded exponentially for the rest of his life. The father of that spiritual family was Captain J.P.A. Mekkes, who had wisely mentored Hans at Stanislau and closely guided his study of a Dooyeweerdian approach to Christian philosophy at Neubrandenburg. Mekkes did not abandon him when they returned to Holland but kept in regular touch with him and nurtured him in every way, spiritually and intellectually, and probably emotionally as well, by his firm friendship.

Presumably it was Mekkes who helped him find a church where he could be baptized. Soon after his return to the Netherlands, Hans was baptized and confirmed and became a member of the Reformed Churches (Vrijgemaakt/Liberated). He later related that while his older sisters had been baptized as babies, his parents had totally forgotten to have him baptized as an infant. Mekkes also quickly helped set him on his way academically by encouraging him to develop and elaborate his thoughts on aesthetics that he had begun to set down at Neubrandenburg. These were brought to fruition and published in two parts in the Calvinist journal *Philosophia Reformata* (1946–1947).

Hans's commitment to the church and his new Christian family did not supplant all of his former friendships. As he tried to reestablish relationships, one person stands out above all others in her openness to Hans and her openness to the faith that he had found while a prisoner of war. This was Anna Marie (nicknamed Anky) Huitker (1915–2003).

Anky was seven years older than Hans. Before the war she had also been a part of his circle of friends and a close personal friend of Riki's. Anky and Riki worked in the same clerical office. They may have become friends at work. Anky knew Riki's family well and socialized with her brothers. When as a mutual friend of Riki and Hans she considerately reported to him in late August 1942 that Riki and her family had been taken away by the Nazis, she had no idea in mind that her relationship with Hans would ever deepen beyond what it was then.

After the scourge and affliction of the war, a new reality emerged. So many loved ones were dead or gone. There was no going back to the good old days, even if they could be called that. There were choices. One could go crazy or become cynical and/or radicalized. One could also squarely face the new terms that life set forth and try to continue to live in as positive and healthy a way as possible. Both Hans and Anky, individually and eventually mutually, gradually did just that. Rather than run away from the new conditions of their lives, they embraced them and moved forward cautiously and circumspectly.

Anky Huitker was a completely different type of woman and personality from Riki Spetter, but of no less character. She was born on August 10, 1915, on the sugar plantation Sindanglaoet, located near the city of Cirebon on the north coast of Java. In 1908, three years before Hans's parents were married, her parents, Leendert (nicknamed Leen) and Maria Helena (nicknamed Lien), moved there. Anky's father managed the sugar refinery located at Sindanglaoet. Anky joined an older sister, Adriana (nicknamed Addy), who had been born in 1911. Their parents were members of the Dutch Reformed Churches (Hervormde Kerk), the major Protestant denomination in the Netherlands that dated back to the sixteenth century, when the northern provinces of the Low Countries revolted against Spanish rule. The symmetry of Anky's and Hans's experience of their earliest years in the Dutch Indies extends to her parents' neglecting to have her baptized as a small child. Perhaps the colonial environment did not lend itself to this sort of conscientiousness or conformity.

Business and management must have been naturally inculcated in the Huitker family. After the family's return to the Netherlands when Anky was still a child, she gravitated in her adolescence to organizational work and found employment in office work. Without a doubt, her true métier was to be an entrepreneur, as would be evident later in her life. She was a person who knew how to get things done. She was petite and wholesomely attractive. She was multilingual, bright and quick, and determined when she sensed a challenge. She was a woman of practical intelligence, but not an intellectual. She also was not a conventionally domestic type of woman, though quite able to manage a household adeptly. She had remarkable tenacity, especially for causes in which she believed.

An amorphous family adherence to Protestantism did not give Anky or her sister, Addy, clear spiritual direction for their lives. After the Great War, thoughts of inevitable human progress and perfection that had insinuated significantly into European thought were severely shattered. The theological liberalism of the churches was on a tremendous roll, undercutting clear commitment to a historical understanding and affirmation of the

Christian faith. There was a virtual vacuum of constructive ideas for fresh spiritual or political or social life at this time. Into this void the West opened itself in an exceptional way to Eastern thought. The Huitker sisters were sensitive and open to these trends of the time.

In the years between the wars they found their way to Castle Eerde near Ommen, where the famous mystic Jiddu Krishnamurti had been invited in 1926 by Baron van Pallandt to make his European home and where thousands flocked to hear him speak. Dutch radio broadcasted his talks. Addy and Anky came from nearby Lemelerveld, where they had first lived after returning from the Dutch Indies and where they still had relatives whom they visited. It was only half an hour at most by bicycle to Eerde to see and hear the charismatic young man known as "The Star of the East," whom Theosophists claimed was the reincarnation of Jesus. There was considerable excitement around the activities at the castle.

Addy, as the older sister, seems to have been influenced more by the atmosphere surrounding Castle Eerde. She kept pictures of herself taken with Krishnamurti. Anky never forgot the experience of being there either. She would have been only fourteen years old when Krishnamurti dramatically announced before an astounded audience of mainly Theosophists that he renounced that he thought or ever considered himself to be a reincarnation of Lord Maitreya, whom most of them believed had been an earlier incarnation of Jesus.

After this admission, the Krishnamurti following at Castle Eerde at Ommen dwindled. A few years later Baron van Pallandt resumed the proprietorship of the castle and made it available from 1933 to Jewish children fleeing persecution by the Nazis, a cause that the Huitker sisters had great sympathy with and that could well have been an important reason why they maintained an attraction for and sympathy with Eerde and never forgot it. It could also have been part of what inspired them to their courageous activities of protecting Jews during the war. Castle Eerde and the camp at Westerbork (known as the Dutch "Gateway to Auschwitz"), locations originally developed as well-organized refuges for Jews fleeing Nazi Germany, were, with cynical pragmatism, commandeered malevolently by the Nazis after their occupation of the Netherlands and used as penal/transit camps for the duration of the war.

Hans and Anky resumed their acquaintance in a gradual and natural way following the war. They both had a concern to find Riki, fiancée and friend. They both had experienced a great deal of hardship and uncertainty during the war years. Anky was no stranger to Nazi terror. In different but equally true ways, Anky's spirit matched Hans's. The Huitker family valiantly united to resist the Nazi occupiers and courageously conspired together at great personal risk for each of them to hide Jews in their home for the duration of the war. Without a letup they lived under constant strain for years. After the war, Addy married Leo Wolff, one of the *onderduikers* who had hidden in their home. A certain nervous tenseness from these years of unwavering vigilance never totally left Anky, though she could, as occasion arose, relax and enjoy herself. From terrible tensions and disintegrated dreams fine filaments of mutual understanding and respect incrementally grew into strong cords of love and commitment between Anky and Hans that were to sustain them for the rest of their lives.

Anky was spiritually hungry and open as she began to see more and more of Hans. He, of course, was eager for her to find the reality of faith in Jesus Christ that he had discovered while a prisoner of war. The message that had fallen on closed ears in his family, she slowly received with warmth and sincerity as he shared it with her and engaged her questions. She neither rushed into faith nor took it lightly. Though they were in contact soon after the war and presumably talked about issues of belief then, it was not until probably sometime in 1947 that her commitment to the Christian faith was clear and defined. She still waited until 1949 (the year in which she and Hans were married) to be baptized and to become a member of the Reformed Church (Vrijgemaakt/Liberated) in Amsterdam.

Hans and Anky showed admirable restraint in their developing relationship. They enjoyed each other's company and companionship, and they were each growing in their Christian faith. They spent time with each other naturally and with ease. Although it seemed likely that Riki had died at Auschwitz, they had no conclusive proof of this. Their reluctance to rush their relationship bore strong signs of having been motivated by respect for someone they both honored and hoped would somehow reappear. Neither Hans nor Anky ever learned that Riki died at Auschwitz on September 30, 1942, shortly after she was taken away. Stalwartly they carried on with their lives and did not make special demands on each other, or life in general for that matter. Anky continued in her office work. Hans pursued his further studies.

Hans's love of learning only increased through his discovery of his love for God. As immediate as his finding Christian affiliation on his return to the Netherlands was, so was his seeking a place where he could continue his education. Thus in 1946, without skipping a beat and with hardly a cent to his name, he enrolled as a student at the University of Amsterdam.

In many ways it was easier for Hans to know his calling as a scholar than it was for him to find the right subject to study, one that could lead to a meaningful career that would provide support for the family he one day hoped to have. Issues that are often the last for a serious scholar to acknowledge were ones that Hans confronted at the outset, even before he had started his university studies.

Czeslaw Milosz, the acclaimed Polish poet and University of California at Berkeley professor, a slightly older contemporary of Hans, points out in his own intellectual and spiritual self-portrait: "A man must abide somewhere, a physical roof over his head is not enough; his mind needs its bearings, its points of reference, vertically as well as horizontally." Often it is in the midst of particular studies that have captivated interest, or even afterward, that a scholar finds his or her intellectual abode. Milosz is an example of someone who eventually consciously and confidently found his abode in the Roman Catholic Christian tradition.

With his conversion Hans recognized immediately his spiritual and intellectual dwelling place to be in a biblical and Reformed tradition. The Christian philosophy of Herman Dooyeweerd was confirmed for him by its high degree of congruence with Scripture, especially in its understanding of God's law perceived in the broadest sense of its co-inherence with the structure of reality. He had not discovered this philosophy and then read it all back into the Bible. Quite the reverse was true. His reading of the Bible prepared him to recognize a way of thinking that could open up biblical insight into the world, scholarly disciplines, and normal human activities. He was not entrapped or enslaved by this philosophy but rather set free. Instead of being scattered in his thinking, he was given aid to think rigorously in a systematic but dynamic way, across categories, without losing his intellectual or spiritual footing, because he had a place to stand. However, for all its benefit to him, it did not provide him with a tidy formula for a career. The questions remained: What specifically was he going to study? What kind of career would his choice create?

Detachment was not a characteristic Hans Rookmaaker exhibited. He was always engaged personally in what he thought and did. In *Aesthetica: structuuranalyse van het muzikale kunstwerk*, the study he began at Neubrandenburg, he managed to pack all his passions for music, philosophy, and a biblical worldview into his formulation. Long before one talked of "personal knowledge" in the Polanyian sense, Hans was intuiting this. Dooyeweerd's philosophy rescued him from Kantian incertitude regarding knowing and alerted him to questioning radically the objectivity and neutrality of any subject, including science. Being personal in one's approach to knowledge did not mean being subjective or creating truth, as in some postmodern trends, but acknowledging one's personal participation in the process of knowing. Hans needed a subject to which he felt close.

Dooyeweerd also made Hans aware of how easily almost any area of human endeavor can become a substitute for religion. In the all-consuming task and fascination of graduate and doctoral studies, many a scholar becomes more the worshiper of his or her subject than its steward or servant. Hans cast about to find a field he could serve.

Music had been his passion. He loved classical music and African-American music, and he knew a great deal about both. Musicology seemed to him an ideal subject. In high hopes of pursing the history of music, he was disappointed when he was told that he did not have the technical prerequisites required for this study. Independently he had studied Greek and Latin, subjects he knew would be required, but he did not realize he needed to be able to play a musical instrument competently to be admitted to a degree in musicology. Ironically, for all his knowledge and appreciation of music, Hans could not make music. For that matter, he could not sing or even carry a tune in the midst of voluminous support during congregational hymn singing. Thus it was that he eventually turned to the study of art history, a subject that he was more than adequately suited to and one that permitted him quite compatibly to continue his serious and abiding interest in African-American music history.

Hans needed to attend to practical matters before he launched into his newfound academic field at the University of Amsterdam. He applied for and was granted a discharge from his commission as a naval officer. He also supervised his mother's move from The Hague to Amsterdam, where he installed her in a flat they shared. At about the same time Addy Huitker married Leo Wolff and moved to Amsterdam. Following this event, Anky and her parents also moved to Amsterdam. In terms of convenience this meant that Hans and Anky were able to see much more of each other.

As though life was not full enough with the responsibilities of study, home and church life, and his growing involvement with and love for Anky, Hans took on the further task of starting a group for Christian students from the Free University and the University of Amsterdam. After beginning his studies, he quickly discerned the need for Christian students, especially those coming from his church, to have strong support in the midst of a university environment that frequently was hostile to their faith and was more inclined to uphold a secular humanism.

Hans was intrinsically mission-minded. He understood that taking a Christian message into the world was as much about sharing it stratigraphically, throughout the academic disciplines and professions at home, as it was about spreading it geographically, abroad. Gathering together students from the Reformed Churches (Vrijgemaakt/Liberated), he gave leadership and helped pioneer the formation of the Vereniging van Gereformeerde Studenten in Amsterdam (VGSA). This fellowship encouraged friendships that nurtured Christian maturity through Bible study and reflection, bringing biblical thought to bear on the issues of life and learning. For the rest of his studies and for the rest of his career, Hans in one way or another supported VGSA and its mission. In appreciation, he in turn was honored by being made a lifelong member.

In 1948 Anky began administrative work in Amsterdam that suited her and brought a friendship to her and Hans that would make a deep impact on both of them and take them to activities and places they could never have dreamed of then. Apparently through church links she had found a job working for the organizing committee preparing for the first and founding assembly of the International Council of Christian Churches (ICCC), held August 11–19, 1948. Under the leadership of Carl McIntire (1906–2002), who had started the Bible Presbyterian Church in 1938 and the American Council of Churches in 1940, delegates from fifty-eight churches representing twenty-nine countries came together to witness to the Lordship of Jesus Christ and to protest against the establishment of the World Council of

Churches (WCC) that was to occur (August 19-September 4, 1948), also in Amsterdam. In McIntire's eyes and probably in the eyes of most of the delegates to the ICCC, the WCC represented the archfiend of liberalism.

Hans was only twenty-six and not exactly an experienced churchman at this stage, nor was he an official delegate to the ICCC meeting. He was a full-time university student who checked in intermittently with the young woman working in the office, namely Anky Huitker, whom he had recently asked to marry him. Later comments by Hans suggest that he did attend some of the sessions. Short of pestering Anky, he was eager to have her find any Americans at the assembly who might know something about African-American music and be willing to talk with him about it.

In the midst of her administrative duties, Anky saw a fair amount of an approachable American who spent time in the ICCC office making special arrangements for various sessions. He had impressed her, and she thought he might be the right man for Hans to speak with. So it was on an evening in August 1948 when Hans accompanied Anky back to her office for her to do some more work that they unexpectedly ran into Francis A. Schaeffer (1912–1984), the very person she wanted Hans to meet, busily working away there. Little did the three of them know at that time the great influence they would have on each other or how their futures would be woven together for the benefit of many people they did not know then or who were not even yet born.

Immediately upon being introduced, Hans respectfully asked Schaeffer, ten years his senior, if he had some time to speak with him. Anky remembered Schaeffer looking at his watch and telling Hans he could spare about half an hour. Then they disappeared to talk. Anky never saw Hans for the rest of the evening. When she saw him the next day, she asked whether his questions had been answered. She was amazed to hear that he never even got around to asking them because he and Schaeffer had gone immediately into an extensive discussion of modern art and its presuppositions that did not end until 4:00 A.M.

The year before the inauguration of the ICCC in Amsterdam, Schaeffer had spent three months traveling throughout Europe as a representative of the Independent Board for Presbyterian Foreign Missions and as the American Secretary for the Foreign Relations Department of the American Council of Christian Churches. He had recently moved to Lausanne, Switzerland with his wife, Edith, and their three young daughters, primarily in order to establish a ministry called Children for Christ. Along with this work he also collaborated from his European base of operations in the formation of the ICCC.

Less than a year after the ICCC assembly in Amsterdam, Hans and Anky were married. If meeting Francis Schaeffer sparked a key event in Hans's life, it also did that for Anky, for whom hearing Schaeffer preach in a way that was understandable and edifying during those days of the ICCC in 1948 contributed greatly to her Christian growth and maturity. As they prepared to enter into the most solemn and momentous commitment of their lives, Anky was probably more acutely aware than Hans was of their lack of family Christian heritage and the need for resources to sustain mutual solidarity for a lasting marriage. Schaeffer's encouragement could well have been what she needed in her spiritual development to help her feel prepared to take such a serious step.

On Wednesday, June 1, 1949 Hans and Anky were married in a civil ceremony attended only by their immediate families at the Town Hall of Amsterdam. A small church service followed later in the week. The little gathering consisted basically of the elders of the church, a few friends from the congregation, and members of the VGSA. The bridal pair was so impoverished that they walked from their little loft in the Huitkers' house to the church for the ceremony. Afterward there was no party, though they did manage to scrape up enough cash to spend a honeymoon in France, visiting Paris, Versailles, and Dijon.

In 1949 European economic recovery from the war was still shaky. Hans and Anky were extremely vulnerable financially, as were their families and most of their peers. Hans found the funds to travel to France and tide them over by selling a valuable stamp collection that he had inherited from his grandfather. Happily, he was able to find income by becoming an art critic for *Trouw*, a daily Dutch newspaper with a strong Calvinist readership coming out of the Kuyperian Christian Reformed (Gereformeerde) tradition. In 1949 he also passed his *kandidaats* examination (equivalent to a Bachelor's degree) and received an appointment as an assistant to Professor I.Q. van Regteren Altena (1899–1980), a connoisseur and specialist in the art of the sixteenth and seventeenth centuries and one of the editors of the prestigious art-historical journal, *Oud Holland*.

Hans wasted no time getting started on both his further studies and a family. As Anky was well into her thirties when they married, they were happy to learn a few months into their marriage that they were expecting a child. As the new baby gestated, so did the new scholar.

Being a graduate assistant had its advantages besides helping cover fees. First of all, it allowed Hans to see more of his professor in action. Secondly, it allowed him to receive more attention from his professor. Thirdly, it gave him invaluable experience in teaching even as he was learning. Van Regteren Altena taught his students to look meticulously at works of art in order to get thoroughly acquainted with them. He also emphasized at the same time the study of them in their art-historical context. Hans was given an excellent apprenticeship in connoisseurship by his professor, who at the time of his studies was also the Director of the Print Room of the Rijksmuseum. Hans's art-historical education was founded on constant exposure to original works of art under expert guidance.

To this erudite and classical formation he added an extraordinary self-education in contemporary art. His reviews for *Trouw* required regular visits to art exhibitions and museums all over the country and occasionally abroad. Although many of the shows he saw were of older art, there was also a burgeoning of modern art to be seen. The young man who had independently cultivated a discerning taste for the nuances of African-American music and a considerable knowledge of its development now applied these same kinds of sensibilities to understanding the visual art of his own era. As both the history of jazz and modern art are now established academic subjects, it needs to be pointed out that when Hans began writing about these subjects in the early 1950s, they were not universally recognized as scholarly subjects. His own contribution in this area, at least in the Netherlands, helped them gain serious attention.

Hans was building his unique blend of competencies. Alongside his technical expertise in art history and firsthand familiarity with contemporary art, he was beginning to hone his ability to communicate with a wide public without pandering to the lowest common denominator of his audience. Furthermore, he was thoroughly imbued with biblical understanding that did not remain locked in a text but dynamically sought a horizon in everyday life.

In his reviews, his style was simple and direct. He knew how to hook his readers' interest in his first paragraph, if not his first line. He always informatively gave historical, cultural, or religious background information that aided his analysis. Without a hint of patronizing, his reviews registered warmth and an undisguised desire to teach and persuade his audience to take action. They are studded with exhortations to "take a closer look," "go see," "take a trip," "hop on a train."

The fashioning of Hans's career and communication skills was well underway when he faced the steepest learning curve that he had encountered up to that point in his life. In Amsterdam, on July 15, 1950, he became a father for the first time. Hans and Anky welcomed a healthy baby boy on that day and named him, in the Rookmaaker family tradition of father and grandfather, Henderik Roelof (Hans/Hansje as he was subsequently nicknamed). Hansje cleverly managed to make his appearance into the world on the date of Rembrandt's birth in 1606.

The new little creature fascinated Hans, but he was not quite sure what to do with it or how to relate to it. Being the slightly spoiled baby in his own family had not helped him have natural intuition for this new situation. His somewhat emotionally distant relationship with his own parents was also an impairment.

After a break of slightly less than three years, Leendert Cornelis (nicknamed Kees), born February 21, 1953, closely followed by Maria Helena (nicknamed Marleen), born August 26, 1954, joined their older brother Hansje. Both of these children were also born in Amsterdam. This time, however, names were chosen from the Huitker side of the family, with Kees being the namesake of his maternal grandfather and Marleen that of her maternal grandmother. Though Hans loved his children dearly and was solicitous of their welfare, he still was not adept at relating to small children and left them almost completely in the hands of their mother as he focused on his studies and writing.

Hans was by no means hopeless as a father. Gradually as the children grew up and he could converse with them, he worked as hard as he could to understand them. Although not emotionally demonstrative, he could be playful and warmly humorous with them. Even if he was not home every evening for a meal, he was faithful in having some family time with them each Sunday afternoon as well as making sure there was an annual vacation. Sometimes during vacations, however, family time was not separated from his personal and professional interests. There was always something he was interested in seeing either on the way or while the family was on holiday. Revolt occurred. Marleen distinctly remembers a period of time when she refused to go into art museums.

In teen years, when many parents try to clamp down strictly on their offspring, Hans wisely listened to his children and left them free to find their way. They continue to respect him for this. Hans never rebuked them for the length of their hair, the clothes they wore, or the music to which they listened. He did not send all his children to Christian schools. Although Hans, Junior did attend a Christian school, Kees and Marleen did not. Hans, who as a teenager had been more than an avid, almost obsessive record collector, had great sympathy with the importance of serious popular music giving direction in his children's lives. They in turn kept him in touch with current trends, even as he was able to show them some of the roots of rock music in jazz and the blues. Hans and Anky did not convey their beliefs and values to their children so much by overt lessons or preaching as by their inherent character and quality of life.

Hans's stamina for work in the 1950s was staggering. As his young family was growing, so was he academically. In the same year that Kees was born (1953), he received his *doctoraal* (equivalent to a Master's degree) in art history from the University of Amsterdam. When he completed his degree, his assistantship also came to an end and, though still writing one or two articles a week for *Trouw*, he needed to regroup and find more income to support his family. For the next three years he took up teaching high school at the Spinoza Lyceum in Amsterdam. All the while he and Anky faithfully supported their church, encouraged students, and hosted a regular Bible study group.

But it was hard going. Because Hans and Anky had not grown up in the church, they felt to a certain extent like outsiders. Anky, especially, felt disappointed and spiritually dry. People outside of the church—her parents, for example—were often more humane than those inside it. A bright spot was their flourishing friendship with Francis and Edith Schaeffer, whom they met with on the Schaeffers' periodic visits to the Netherlands.

Anky took particular interest in their ministry to children and the Bible study lessons they prepared for them. When asked by the Schaeffers to help with this work in Holland, Anky found it benefited her as much as it did her own children and their friends who came into her home.

These same years were not easy for the Schaeffers either. In the summer of 1954 their young son, Franky, contracted polio. Early in 1955 the Swiss government notified them that they had to leave the country permanently within six weeks. Astonishingly, a turnabout of this situation occurred through a set of unusual circumstances when they acquired unexpected funding to purchase Chalet les Mèlézes in Huémoz and were allowed to remain in Switzerland. Anky and Hans, who kept in close contact with and constant prayer for them, rejoiced at the reversal of events and followed with exceeding interest the transformation of the Schaeffers' ministry after their season of crisis. On June 4, 1955, Francis Schaeffer resigned from the Independent Board for Presbyterian Foreign Missions and inaugurated the informal beginning of L'Abri Fellowship, a work of hospitality and hope that gave shelter (the French word *L'Abri* means "shelter") to countless numbers of spiritually and intellectually hungry seekers.

That summer, with three small children aged five and under, Hans and Anky set off to see their friends in Switzerland. Anky never forgot their first visit to Huémoz. Meals were marvelous times of feeding body and soul as they lingered over dinner in deep discussion about all the things that meant the most to her and Hans. It almost made her forget that she had on her hands three small rascally Rookmaakers, as full of energy as their father had ever been as a child. She appreciated Mrs. Schaeffer's graciously doing her best to cater to these little creatures when they turned up their noses at ice cream and cakes and called for bread and milk. Monolinguals can have little comprehension of how bewildering it is for children to be surrounded by a swirl of adults speaking a language other than their own. All three Rookmaaker children seem to have survived their initiation into English by subsequently learning to speak it with exceptional fluency.

Hans and Anky came away from their visit to Huémoz spiritually refreshed and inspired, despite being a little ragged around the edges from managing their healthy young brood on such a long excursion. Not too many months later they decided to cut to the quick and go for a future that would prepare Hans to engage at the highest levels the kinds of seekers that came to a place like L'Abri. In 1956 Hans finished his work with *Trouw* and turned his focus full-time to obtaining a doctorate in art history, at the same time struggling with his burning desire to write a book on jazz, blues, and spirituals.

Hans drove himself harder than ever. He was back at the University of Amsterdam with his old professor, van Regteren Altena. He loved the art of the sixteenth and seventeenth centuries, but he felt a tremendous pull toward understanding the art of the century in which he lived. He was convinced by everything he had experienced so far in his life that the crisis of the modern condition, which had reaped chaos and devastation for most of the twentieth century, could be understood through modern art, which presented a way of disclosing what was at stake in assuming the validity of modernity's presuppositions. The powers of persuasion with which he charmed his *Trouw* readers must have worked on his professor as he made the case for a dissertation on Paul Gauguin and Synthetist art theories as a critical bridge between the art of the ages, as it were, and what was created in the twentieth century.

Graham Birtwistle, in his fine essay on the shaping of Rookmaaker's thought, makes clear that few established academics at the time deemed modern art a true task for a real scholar. That Hans along with his contemporary, Hans Jaffé, curator at the Stedelijk Museum of Amsterdam, who investigated the De Stijl movement of the 1920s, were allowed to research areas of modern art affirms that the faculty of art history at Amsterdam was willing to move beyond its reputation for impeccable historical scholarship to a progressive consideration of more recent art. It put Hans in the vanguard of what the Dutch art-historical establishment was willing to concede as serious research.

On the practical side, teaching at a high school, no matter

how fine the students were or how prestigious the institution, could not drive forward his scholarship or his career. Providentially he was able to find a new position that undergirded his studies, expanded his art-historical horizons, prepared him professionally to be competitive for a future job market, and provided him with income.

Moving from *Trouw* into his doctoral work, Hans found a position in 1957 as assistant to Professor Henri (Hans) van de Waal (1910–1972) at the University of Leiden while he was still living in Amsterdam. One is tempted to wonder what bonds of tacit sympathy there might have been between Hans and van de Waal, a Jew who was dismissed from his position as assistant at the Leiden Print Collection at the time of the Nazi occupation of the Netherlands. Van de Waal somehow managed to escape far worse from the occupiers' hands and returned after the war to become both the director of the Print Collection and a professor of art history at the University of Leiden. The great Polish Catholic Christian art historian Jan Bialostocki called van de Waal "one of the masters of the study of images."

Although Hans never earned a degree from his work at Leiden, nor ever intended to, it is safe to say he learned as much there by assisting van de Waal as if he had earned a second doctorate. As a scholar of Dutch historical iconography of the sixteenth to the eighteenth centuries in its relation to religion, literature, and social history, van de Waal pioneered the systematization of iconological groups as they relate to specific typological contexts. This was one of the greatest boons those studying the content and meaning of historical art could have hoped for, as it made collections of art works readily accessible on the basis of subject, not just by artist or more general categories such as landscape, portrait, or still life. Working with the thousands of photo cards of artworks amassed by the Rijksbureau voor Kunsthistorische Documentatie (RKD/ Netherlands Institute for Art History, founded in 1932), van de Waal designed an ingenious system of number/letter/code classification called the Decimal Index of Art of the Low Countries

(DIAL), which he presented in 1958. To make his system more easily available to international scholars, van de Waal chose English. The system was so successful that an improved and extended version of DIAL that no longer focused only on Dutch art was published in 1968. It is called the Iconclass System.

During most of the decade of the development of Iconclass, Hans was van de Waal's right-hand man at Leiden until his own appointment as professor of art history at the Free University of Amsterdam. Rookmaaker's loyalty is confirmed in his correspondence. He did not want to run away from his work at Leiden and leave his older colleague in the lurch. At pains to give proper closure to his time there, he recruited and trained his successor amidst preparations to take up his own post. One assumes this was Leendert D. Couprie, who eventually succeeded van de Waal and went on to edit and complete the Iconclass system when the scholar of images died in 1972. Rookmaaker's calendars show he continued to keep in regular contact with Couprie well into the 1970s after van de Waal's death.

While Rookmaaker shows evidence of being influenced by art historians such as Hans Sedlmayr, Erwin Panofsky, and Ernst Gombrich, a less explicit but much deeper influence may have been van de Waal. The deviser of DIAL/Iconclass may not be as well known as those other scholars are, but he was equally as great and in many ways a more multifaceted scholar and educator. The model van de Waal provided Rookmaaker with in their close working relationship should not be overlooked as an important influence on him. Van de Waal kept up cordial collegial relations with many leading art historians, including Panofsky and Fritz Saxl of the Warburg Institute in London. He founded a special collection on the History of Photography as one of the divisions of the Leiden Print Collection. He was an outstanding lecturer and much loved as a teacher by his students, both of art history and other disciplines. He was committed to art education for young people, a concern that led to his being made the Dutch delegate to UNESCO seminars on the role of museums in education. R. H. Fuchs said of him, "the history of art, in his experience, was not just an area of human endeavour to be documented, mapped, analyzed and interpreted. To him it meant, above all, the opportunity to study how individuals function within their culture, and, conversely, how a culture nurtures and shapes an individual."

Those familiar with Rookmaaker's own breadth of interests should not have trouble seeing how van de Waal's approach would have appealed to him and implicitly influenced his emphasis on the content of art in its cultural context and gave him ideas about the scope of what can be included and brought to bear on the understanding of works of art. Fuchs's further description of van de Waal helps us see this better.

> [Van de Waal] remained aloof from the doctrinaire and the bullying. In an ancient Jewish tradition, he was not a teacher of a discipline, but a teacher for individuals. That is why he firmly refused to conduct a course in methodology; he instinctively felt that by doing so he would limit his students' personal freedom and hinder the development of their individual talents. He did, though, conduct a graduate seminar in what he called beeldleer—the 'general science of images', related to art as linguistics is to literary texts. Definitely not a methodology or a theory of art, van de Waal's beeldleer was more like a systematic inventory of everything that conditions a work of art, from the properties of paint to iconographic codes and from the history of frames to the history of taste. Beeldleer precedes methodology; it deals not with schematic structures but with concrete, particular facts.

Van de Waal's decision to set up DIAL/Iconclass in English may also have influenced Hans's decision to go the harder route and write his dissertation on Gauguin in English so that it could reach a wider academic audience. As doctoral research goes, he completed his work in record time, especially considering that he was holding down a job to support his family as well as working on writing another book at the same time. At 4:00 P.M. on July 7, 1959, he went to his *promotie* (graduation ceremony) at the University of Amsterdam. He got there by the skin of his teeth.

The successful candidate for the *doctoraat*, H.R. Rookmaaker, and his dear wife who had supported him all the way by keeping the home fires burning and typing his drafts and their corrections must have been greatly relieved. This time after the ceremony there was a party. Van Regteren Altena, Hans's professor, wrote the next day to say thank you for the enjoyable, presumably expansive meal and evening he had had with him and Anky and others after the official conferring on of the doctoral degree.

In *Synthetist Art Theories*, Hans's dissertation on Paul Gauguin, he broke new ground for the study of the dynamics of thought and artistic practice at play at the inception of modern art. Sifting through a monumental amount of nineteenth-century French art theory and selecting, translating, and analyzing pertinent texts have won Rookmaaker regard for decades. To this he added an analysis of Gauguin's contribution as a major figure who fought for the artist's freedom to find new forms apart from any previously held established tradition, conceived an understanding of the iconic character of the visual arts (that is, color and line representation of the visible world can express what is unseen but equally as real), and created a new and higher value for the decorative aspects of art.

In the days before Rookmaaker's *promotie* all of his hard work and original research hung in the balance. The committee from the Faculty of Arts and Letters was not convinced that he had written a text that was in comprehensible English. Hans was the first to admit that his English was not perfect. Yes, he had made the decision to write in English. Days before he was to defend his work, he was asked in a threatening way to translate everything into Dutch. Seeing this problem coming, he had called upon his friends, who came to his rescue. Both Calvin Seerveld and Francis Schaeffer wrote letters to the committee, stating that though *Synthetist Art Theories* was not written in perfect English, it was clear, scholarly discourse in English and they should approve his dissertation. Schaeffer, in his letter, added that not only had he read the manuscript, he'd had a Cambridge scholar who was visiting him also read Rookmaaker's writing, and both agreed that it could be understood. That may have clinched it for the committee. It surely added further bonds to an already established friendship, as well as a deep debt of gratitude to Seerveld for help in the hour of need.

One has the sense that Rookmaaker sought his Ph.D. in the way one would a union card or a valuable ticket to a game or concert. He was interested in his subject and knew it added to knowledge about the emergence of modern art, which he was passionate about understanding. But completing this goal over these years was not the all-consuming end to which he was willing to sacrifice his soul and other interests or commitments in his life as often happens with graduate students on a trajectory to having a brilliant career. He remained committed to VGSA, his involvement with L'Abri deepened, he spoke at churches and conferences and student groups, he remained faithful to his circle for Bible study, and he continued writing his book on jazz, blues, and spirituals. Though he was quite serious about his research, one almost has the feeling that his dissertation was a nuisance he had to get through in order to do other things to which his broader vision of mission and life called him.

Near to his heart was a project that he had dreamed of and nurtured for a long time. This was his book *Jazz, Blues, Spirituals* (1960). Even as he was in the last throes of writing his dissertation, he was lining up details regarding publication permissions for this book. It must have been the book he had wanted to write since he was a boy.

In 1958, prior to the completion of Hans's doctorate, the Rookmaaker family moved to Leiden. By the time of the publication of *Synthetist Art Theories* and *Jazz, Blues, Spiritual*s, they were domestically well established there. As he settled into teaching at Leiden and working with DIAL/Iconclass, Hans seems to have known, however, that he would not be spending the rest of his academic career there. By this time there is also the sense that he liked the intensity of doing many things at the same time. Soon he applied for and was granted funding by the Dutch government to travel to the United States for the purpose of learning how art history was taught there. It provided a special opportunity to spy out the land to see if he might have a professional future there. Professorships in art history were much more limited in number in the Netherlands than they were in North America.

On August 27, 1961, the day after his daughter Marleen's seventh birthday, Hans flew to New York, where he was welcomed by Harry Schat, a Dutch friend of his living in New Jersey. Harry was a multilingual businessman with an ardent bent for Reformed theology. Hans and Anky had known him for years. In fact, he was the son-in-law of Dominee Meester, the minister who had baptized Anky. Harry was a born organizer and helped get Hans on the road immediately, first to Toronto and then all around the eastern USA. Until December 14, when Hans flew back to the Netherlands, he kept up a grueling pace, meeting literally hundreds of people, visiting every major art collection from the northeast seaboard to the Midwest, attending the College Art Association meeting in New York City, contacting dozens of prominent art historians, and seeing at least twenty college and university campuses. He also took this opportunity to make connections with numerous leading figures from the African-American community.

He returned home nearly physically exhausted but mentally restless. He went back to his regular routines of teaching, rounds of speaking, and, with Anky, commitment to L'Abri. But soon he was inquiring about all kinds of job possibilities in the USA and asking his American friends for their advice regarding the academic credibility of various institutions and which ones would be better for a position. He cast his net so wide that he was even

willing to teach philosophy (a field he had no professional qual-
ification in) rather than art history. In one or two instances, such
as at the University of Rhode Island, his negotiations became
quite advanced. Probably gnawing at the back of his mind was
how in future days he was going to support his family adequately
continuing on only a lecturer/assistant's salary and that he ought
to make contingencies for their provision. He had sold his grandfather's stamp collection when he needed to. He also was willing
to sell some of his rare records, if need be. He made little on his
writing or speaking. The Rookmaakers were by no means financially comfortable during this time of their lives.

It is questionable whether Rookmaaker really wanted to
leave the Netherlands, except for pragmatic reasons. Possibly he
also hoped that if rumors spread that he was about to be hired
for a job in America, he might appear more valuable at home and
some people would not want to lose him.

Whether or not that was the case or merely in his mind, in
late 1963 or early 1964 Rookmaaker was approached by academic representatives of the Free University of Amsterdam who
came to his home in Leiden with an invitation for him to
become the founding professor of a new department of art history. Abraham Kuyper, the Dutch Calvinist theologian and
political leader, founded the Free University in 1880. It was free
in the sense of free from both church and state control as an
independent institution. It was also where Herman Dooyeweerd
taught. As Rookmaaker had never relinquished his active participation in the circles that regularly studied Reformational
thought, particularly Dooyeweerd's, he and Anky accepted the
invitation almost immediately. At last he had found a place
where he could be faithful to his calling as he furthered his
career. He could create and contribute something new within
the Dutch Calvinist ethos that often shied away from serious
engagement with the arts.

In the middle of 1964, the Rookmaakers moved from Leiden
to Diemen, a suburb of Amsterdam not far from the university.

Hans was happy working at the Free University and, at last, enabling the family to own their home. There was an atmosphere of energy around the big city. An added bonus to the move, especially for the children, was the proximity of Grandma Huitker and Aunt Addy and Uncle Leo. They lived just ten minutes away by bicycle, which made it easy for the younger members of the family to see their relatives. Aunt Addy was a good cook, and she and her husband were warm, hospitable people.

The children liked going regularly to the Wolff-Huitker home on Wednesday afternoons and also for *Sinterklaas* (December 5, St. Nicholas Day, when the Dutch traditionally exchange gifts).

Although Anky and Hans did not see eye to eye with Addy and Leo on every matter, they had a cordial relationship with them. Leo was one of the directors of a leading socialist publishing house (Arbeiderspers). Addy was active in volunteering for socialist political causes. They were devoted to each other and, with no children of their own, were generous toward the Rookmaaker children.

The relationship on the other side of the family was still quite ruptured. Hans grappled with varying degrees of estrangement from his siblings for the rest of his life.

It must have pained him not to have close communication with his sisters, whom he had been so near to as a boy and adolescent. They still could not get over the religious commitment he had made and the reinforcement of this in their eyes by his marrying someone who held the same convictions equally firmly. Hans never flagged in his constancy of concern and support for the care of his mother. Whether she was aware of her son's activities and attainments remains uncertain because of her increasing dementia. But she lived to the day her son had become a full professor and best-selling author. At the age of eighty-one she died quietly in The Hague on July 12, 1971.

By this time Hans had been at the Free University for seven years. He was stretched by additional demanding administrative duties, which he'd never had to the same degree at Leiden. He steadily attracted students, and the art history department grew. Internationally he was in high demand as one of the most articulate Christian spokespersons in the world for the arts.

Hans and Anky's support of L'Abri Fellowship also continued to deepen with every passing year. They had a constant flow of seekers through their home. They urged many to go to Swiss L'Abri. Many of these found they felt lost there as the community at Huémoz expanded rapidly in the early 1970s when word spread around the world of its unique atmosphere. The Rookmaakers desired to build up an indigenous Dutch L'Abri to serve the growing numbers coming to them for counsel. From the late 1960s onward they poured enormous effort into this task. And, as though Anky did not have enough to do with this work, out of a vision to feed the hungry and clothe the naked she set out to found an international charitable agency to support orphans and poor children, called Redt een Kind (Save a Child), an organization that has grown and continues to serve. Hans fully supported his wife's humanitarian and entrepreneurial endeavors.

The years of crafting a career and forming a family had been arduous but blessed with twists and turns and full of surprises that Hans could never have surmised when he returned to Holland after the war. There still were heartaches, but there was an even greater abundance of joy. The tapestry of his life was rich. He had a fine family, a career that perfectly matched his calling, and a widening circle of genuine friends.

SIX

FRIENDSHIPS

In the last decade of his life, Rookmaaker's friendships both at home and abroad burgeoned. Amidst the extensive and intensive activities of administrating, teaching, writing, speaking, and traveling, he managed to maintain a high level of consistency in his commitment to his friends, old and new.

The domain of friendship may have been where he was most open. This is surprising because his demeanor was reserved, and he appeared somewhat wary in encounters with new acquaintances. His conservative clothing and pipe puffing reinforced a feeling of his keeping his distance. North Americans often felt intimidated by his Continental, professorial bearing. In this way his style was not "friendly" at all.

Rookmaaker's openness to other people was more profound and far-reaching than immediate amiability. Superficiality was not a part of his makeup. The war and his conversion had set a significant standard for the meaning of friendship, its costliness and its mystery. Looking more closely at some representative friendships and also at some of the circles where he found friendship enables us to see him in ways that otherwise might be overlooked or not evident.

Foundational for all Rookmaaker's postwar friendships was J.P.A. Mekkes, who never ceased to be concerned for Hans's welfare from the time he met him in the Stanislau POW camp to his sudden death in 1977. (Mekkes lived to be ninety, dying ten years after Hans.) Erect and dignified, Mekkes knew how to be more than a regimented military man or a precise philosopher; he knew how to be a warmhearted, faithful friend.

In speaking and writing, Rookmaaker's own reluctance to be overly autobiographical inadvertently has given the impression that Mekkes merely served as a catalyst to his conversion, providentially entering his life, encouraging him to pursue scholarship after the war, and afterward seemingly disappearing from his life. This is far from the case.

It is moving to see Mekkes marching along with Hans through the rest of his life. Hans, in his turn, was not only a receiver of this rich gift but also a generous giver of friendship to Mekkes and many others. In June 1945, not long after both of them had returned to Holland from Neubrandenburg, Mekkes wrote to console Hans regarding his not finding Riki and his almost certainty that she was not alive. He also rejoiced with Hans in his going on to pursue formal studies, and he wished him to have peace once again.

In late May 1959, Mekkes wrote of his happiness at hearing that Hans's *promotie* for his doctorate was moving forward and that all the conversations they'd had in the barracks had not been wasted. He also stated his disappointment and regret at not being able to attend the ceremony because of ill health and his doctor's orders for him to go away for six weeks of curative rest. Rounding out the message the old soldier wrote:

> But our road goes on, and I hope we will [travel] together faithfully for a long time. I hope you have a vacation afterwards. It is good for your family to do this. I didn't do it enough. Now that you have this high point of hard work behind you, you must relax. Greetings to Anky.
>
> > A handshake from your marching companion
> > and colleague,
> > Mekkes

When Mekkes returned from his cure, he and his wife were delighted to find a beautiful flower arrangement sent by Hans and Anky to welcome them home. He let Hans know how much he appreciated the thoughtfulness and effort of this gesture at a time when he must have had many things to think about. He also communicated that he was reading Hans's dissertation by "spoonfuls."

On it went. He cared about all the facets of Hans's life. Mekkes immediately sent his congratulations to both Hans and Anky when he heard that Hans had been nominated as professor of art history at the Free University. He was thrilled that Hans could extend an application of the Philosophy of the Cosmonomic Idea into another area of scholarship and that he was finding his lifework unfold in this way. He was glad Hans could pass his position at Leiden into good hands. He wondered if Hans's mother could grasp her son's achievement, how the children were handling the changes, and whether the family had found the right house to live in.

Although Mekkes undoubtedly influenced Rookmaaker intellectually, the thread of Mekkes's abiding influence in his life was spiritual and most detectable perhaps in the value Hans placed on friendship and the effort he was willing to expend on the quality of a relationship. Hans's friendship with Mekkes did not require frequent personal meetings to sustain it. It was simply a fact of their lives. They loyally remembered each other, whether it was a birthday here or the publication of a book there. If Mekkes's handwriting became feebler over the years, his friendship did not! They shared a bond that broke boundaries and crossed traditional barriers of friendship, enriching Hans immeasurably and ultimately helping him in his relatively few years to be an enormous hope and help to others.

Mekkes was of the generation of Herman Dooyeweerd and Dirk H. Theodoor Vollenhoven, all of whom were also of the generation of C.S. Lewis, Owen Barfield, and J.R.R. Tolkien. They all had experienced the First World War. Mekkes met Rookmaaker with the authority of an experienced higher-ranking officer and informed mentor when Hans was a mere midshipman imprisoned during the Second World War. Although Hans eventually became a faculty member and theoretically equal colleague of both Dooyeweerd and Vollenhoven at the Free University and knew them both, he never experienced their friendship in the same personal way as with Mekkes. There was always a gulf with these luminaries as between initiates and a neophyte, between teachers and a student. Mekkes shared his experience with Hans, but not in a paternalistic way.

It is to Mekkes's credit that he did not allow differences of age (twenty-five years), rank, or expertise to prevent him from transforming an inherently unequal relationship into bonds of reciprocal friendship and collegiality. He did not try to dominate his protégé but released him into a wider world. Mekkes must have understood deeply that Jesus had called his disciples, including himself and Hans, to be friends, not servants or slaves. Hans, for his part, had unfailing respect coupled with love and affection for this unique friend whose ardent adherence to theoretical thought never prevented him from its application to real life and the nurturing of living relationships.

The most well-known and celebrated of Rookmaaker's friendships was with Francis A. Schaeffer. At the height of both their public lives in the late 1960s and early 1970s, few people would have noticed that there was a decade of difference in their ages. The impression was of two highly different personalities with distinct callings focused on a common mission. In appearance the languorous Alpine guru, dressed in long, woolen stockings and corduroy trousers fastened at the knee suitable for mountain climbing, contrasted dramatically with the dapper little Dutch professor, neatly dressed in his three-piece suit and smoking his pipe. Like complementary colors, each giving a distinct hue, they contrasted but also exhibited an organic, underlying affinity. This produced a potent dynamism when they appeared together, as they often did, at L'Abri conferences held in North America and Europe during those years.

Any self-consciousness of the age gap between them must have diminished quickly. From the start Hans, the younger man, was prompting the arts education of the older man as he talked with Schaeffer about the meaning of modern art far into the night on the occasion of their first meeting in 1948. We do not know whether Schaeffer was looking for this kind of intellectual conversation partner. He came to the exchange with Rookmaaker prepared in a way that few, if any, postwar American missionaries to Europe were. He was a regular visitor to art galleries and museums. The rich legacy of European culture was not lost on Schaeffer, and he knew that art mattered in understanding contemporary Continental society as it related to his unfolding ministry in Europe.

Hans, for his part, already had entrée into a circle of serious discussion regarding Christian philosophy and cultural matters that Mekkes had introduced him to before he met Schaeffer. The arts, however, were not fully on the agenda of these Reformational thinkers, although Abraham Kuyper had addressed the place of art in a Calvinist life system in a rectorial address at the Free University (1888) as well as in his famous Stone Lectures on Calvinism given at Princeton Theological Seminary in 1898. Schaeffer must have been familiar with the Stone Lectures from his Reformed theological education in

America, and this could well have opened him to further consideration of the arts when he arrived in Europe.

Almost immediately both Hans and Schaeffer recognized a meeting of minds in the neglected area of Christian reflection on the arts. This domain established their intellectual reciprocity and personal relationship. It by no means defined it or prescribed it. Over the course of the next thirty years their friendship would widen and deepen, be tested and flourish.

From a conventional point of view, they were unlikely candidates for the kind of closeness and camaraderie they developed. Schaeffer was American. He was older. He had experienced World War II at a safe distance. He was an ordained minister. As we have seen, he and his wife had come to Europe for the purpose of ministry to children who had experienced the trauma of war and uncertain postwar conditions. He first was Bible Presbyterian, one of several fundamentalist offshoots from the Presbyterian Church in the USA that started with J. Gresham Machen's secession in 1929 from Princeton Theological Seminary to form Westminster Theological Seminary in Philadelphia. In the 1950s Schaeffer had moved, however, in an evangelical direction when he joined the greater portion of Bible Presbyterians who, opposed to Carl McIntire's narrow leadership, formed the Reformed Presbyterian Church, Evangelical Synod (today part of the Presbyterian Church in America). He was educated, but by no means a scholar.

Rookmaaker, on the other hand, was European. He was younger. In the midst of the upheaval of a terrible war, he had become a Christian. He was more interested in philosophy than theology. He had just become engaged and was still finding his career path when he met Schaeffer. While he too was a member of an offshoot Reformed group (Vrijgemaakt/Liberated, formed in 1944/45), his circles in the Netherlands by no means mirrored those in the USA. Smoking and drinking were not considered taboo. Nor were these Calvinists in Holland entrenched as exclusively in theological debate as Schaeffer's American colleagues were. Many were actively exploring new intellectual terrain opened up by Kuyper's wide-ranging thinking that a Calvinist understanding applied to all realms of life and learning and not just to the theological or ecclesiastical. Furthermore, Rookmaaker had a much more academic bent than Schaeffer.

If they exhibited stark contrasts, they also evidenced strong convergences. Both Schaeffer and Rookmaaker were committed to being faithful to Scripture in its full-orbed holy composition. They also shared a broad missional vision of seeing both individuals and society transformed by the reality of a living and loving God active in the world. If Schaeffer was an evangelist who was an intellectual, Rookmaaker was an intellectual who was an evangelist. Many came to faith through both of them. Neither of them fit the standard profile of an evangelist or an intellectual. Both of them blew apart the common prejudice that being biblical and theologically orthodox meant being culturally irrelevant.

The spiritual hunger of the West that was evident in the appeal and growth of Eastern religions between the world wars resurged in the 1960s. As the passionate desire for political reform was often linked to Marxism and left-wing politics, the religious element appearing in a myriad of forms in the striving for reform during these times often has been overlooked or obscured in hindsight as historical interpretation has stressed the rise of various sociopolitical movements such as civil rights, feminism, and environmental concern. Some ministers (most famously, Martin Luther King, Jr.) gave key leadership to these causes even as they did in previous centuries to the struggle to abolish slavery and to open the way for women's rights. Yet most ministers only observed these occurrences from the sidelines and preached from the safety of their sanctuaries, not truly knowing how to discern the trends of the times or what to do with such an unruly heterodox mixture of belief and protest. Mentors, guides, and gurus were in demand. Many, if not most of them, proved less than reliable. There was also a great longing for community.

Schaeffer and Rookmaaker, despite their different backgrounds, were both able to see that the spiritual quest of the younger generation was not focused only on the religious sphere but also was creating unrest in other areas of cultural life and experience. Their friendship had prepared them in a remarkable way to meet these conditions.

Although their relationship had been sparked initially by intellectual exchange, it was not limited to this realm. Their friendship soon became a rich and complex mix of four people and two couples, all sharing a vision of serving rather than careerism. In a reminiscence of their friendship, Edith Schaeffer looked back in 1977, after Hans's death, to the time they had all met before L'Abri Fellowship had ever even been thought of. She remembered how she and Fran had helped Hans and Anky get bed linens for their first home as rationing was still a fact of life in Holland and made it difficult for a young couple to buy enough basic household goods to get started. Before the establishment of L'Abri, the Rookmaakers joined with their friends to start Children of Christ classes in Europe and supported them when the Schaeffers were in deep difficulties and it looked like they would have no future in Switzerland.

When Swiss L'Abri was formed in 1955, the Rookmaakers were some of the Schaeffers' first guests. The ethos of hope and hospitality they experienced with their friends strengthened the bonds of their appreciation and inspired them to continue and expand their own reception of students and seekers (many of them artists) into their home. The conversations with the Schaeffers may also have been the providential prompt that mobilized the Rookmaakers' resolve for Hans to complete a doctorate. Hans and Anky were struck by how much more prayer there was at L'Abri in comparison with the Dutch Christian circles they were familiar with. Not only did the Rookmaakers become members of the work of L'Abri in Switzerland, but they also exerted themselves at home, so that the momentum from their efforts eventually grew into a full-fledged L'Abri Fellowship in the Netherlands.

By 1971 a huge welcoming, white, eighteenth-century farm-house (Huize Kortenhoeve) at Eck en Wiel in the agriculturally rich province of Gelderland was purchased through the L'Abri Foundation of the Netherlands (Stichting L'Abri Fellowship Nederland). The widening circle of transforming friendship begun in the Rookmaaker home (first in Leiden and then in Amsterdam) could no longer be hosted there, due to lack of space, and a new stage in the work of L'Abri in Holland bur-geoned forth that would shape the Rookmaakers in Hans's last years almost as much as they shaped the work.

Character and conviction were more at the root of Rookmaaker's and Schaeffer's firm friendship than complete intellectual similitude or the parallel shaping of their thought. Schaeffer had the utmost respect for Herman Dooyeweerd, but he also admitted he had been virtually untouched by his formal philosophy. A key component to Schaeffer's apologetic strategy was the presuppositionalist theology of Cornelius Van Til (1895–1987), a professor of theology at Westminster Theological Seminary who in turn had drawn upon Kuyperian critical thought for his formulations. In a letter to Hans in 1967, Schaeffer marveled that although their thinking had developed independently, it flowed in a similar direction. Spiritually and intellectually they were in essential agreement; yet there was an openness in their relationship that allowed for differences and breathed vitality for hundreds, and probably thousands, of young people seeking renewed direction for their lives.

One has sympathy for the tension that Rookmaaker must have felt knowing that his contemporary Dutch friends had done more robust theoretical thinking than his American friend and his offshoot tradition had. But it was also true that his more pre-cise-thinking Reformed comrades had often neglected actual application of their rigorous reflection to contemporary mis-sional engagement in the culture of the day.

Both Rookmaaker and Schaeffer shared a courageously wider view of the world that was not based on a slavish adherence to a cramped consensus of academic opinion or credentials for its interpretation. They both had a bold confidence backed by considerable experiential learning that transcended a need to have academic respectability. They did not mean to flaunt this. They had a mission that was not advanced by finicky correctness for every detail being covered before a word could be said on a subject. Justifiably and unjustifiably, they were often criticized for lack of precision or for generalizations they made about subjects in which they had little expertise. Generally Rookmaaker was more cautious. While the scholarly establishment felt constrained to contain and maintain discrete fields of knowledge and research in the university, students were seething to know how knowledge applied to their yearnings for a different world. In short, they hungered after wisdom as to how they should live. Both Schaeffer and Rookmaaker movingly identified with their spiritual and intellectual longings and communicated this compassionately.

Perhaps because L'Abri Fellowship was outside of formal establishment structures, it created a subversive appeal apropos of the period that was extremely attractive to those seeking holistic meaning in an age of fragmentation. L'Abri (meaning "shelter" in French) gave, and continues to give, refuge literally and figuratively to an enormous number of people. It should not be forgotten that it is also a fellowship, a company and community of friends. L'Abri did not arise from clever leadership using strategic planning to tailor a ministry to meet the needs of the perceived spiritual market of the time, but out of abiding friendship, not only between Schaeffer and Rookmaaker and their spouses, but a host of others as well who worked and frequently struggled to build community rather than a well-oiled organization.

The authenticity of Rookmaaker's and Schaeffer's partnership appealed powerfully to students in the 1960s and 1970s. They had a significant track record of loyalty to each other. Schaeffer encouraged Hans in his doctoral work. When Rookmaaker's dissertation was challenged for being written in stilted and stylistically awkward English by his university committee and threatened with rejection, Schaeffer, along with Calvin Seerveld, came valiantly to his defense so that an exception was made by the committee and the objection was dropped. Meanwhile Rookmaaker, the veteran journalist, urged Schaeffer to write whether he had impressive degrees behind his name or not. In the famous student protest year of 1968, book after book began to flow from Schaeffer. But only he and Hans and a small circle were aware of the adversity in which these publications had arisen. At the beginning of 1967, Schaeffer was depressed and shared what a difficult time it was for him. For some time he had been under siege by a small but adamant sector of Reformed adherents in America with strong links to the Netherlands who were attacking him theologically and philosophically. Much of their criticism centered on Schaeffer's embracing of American evangelicalism. They also censured Schaeffer because they thought he was out of touch with American culture after living in Europe for twenty years. His final failure seemed to have been that in their opinion he did not understand sufficiently Reformational thinking as rendered by Herman Dooyeweerd and others associated with his generation of Dutch Christian philosophy.

These people were also alarmed by what they construed as Schaeffer's overweening influence on Rookmaaker. They let Hans know this with intense persistency, as though they desired to drive a wedge between him and his friend. This placed Hans in a difficult position and jeopardized some relations of long standing that he valued and about which he did not want to declare a choice. He was dismayed by the sharp tone and unloving attitudes of the accusations he heard against his colleague.

Rookmaaker ultimately refused to be intimidated by these tactics and took his stand with Schaeffer. He wrote in a letter to Cornelius Van Til on May 10, 1967 about how irrational he found the attacks on Schaeffer and how much he appreciated the Westminster theologian's not endorsing the views expressed by

Schaeffer's critics. He further explained how his friend had developed his thinking and his own terminology in communicating with a generation that did not lay stress on theological doctrine, which if it had been mentioned would have scared them away from listening. Schaeffer's strategy, he said, was developed "on the battlefield" in discussions with young radicals, existentialists, angry young men, or Christian students on their way to losing their faith because of the pressures of present-day culture. It aimed to convince young people that a biblical Christianity was both relevant and required special commitment.

In covering the criticism of Schaeffer, Rookmaaker wanted to communicate clearly to Van Til that Schaeffer had recently received a friendly welcome from his Dutch Reformational circles. At the end of February and the beginning of March 1967, Schaeffer spent nearly a week with Rookmaaker at the Free University. During this time Schaeffer gave a formal lecture on the background and spiritual principles of modern philosophy that Rookmaaker considered, not surprisingly, in line with Dooyeweerd's thinking. Hans reported to Van Til as well that Schaeffer had had an extended personal visit with Dooyeweerd and that it had gone well. No doubt Hans was hoping Van Til would broadcast all of this on his side of the Atlantic.

Even before this visit Rookmaaker's friends and colleagues at the Free University could have been in little doubt about the impact Schaeffer had had on him. Amidst the opening remarks of his inaugural address as professor of art history at the Free University on May 28, 1965, Rookmaaker directed special words of appreciation to Schaeffer for being there. On the occasion of this significant milestone in his own career, he went on record as to what their relationship meant to him by saying:

> It seems to me a token, not only of our friendship but also of our spiritual unity, that you have come from Switzerland for this occasion. Since the first time we met, in 1948, we have had many long talks about faith, philosophy, reality, art, the

modern world, and their mutual relations. I owe very much to these discussions, which have helped to shape my thoughts on these subjects. I want to express my deep gratitude, and consider it a great honour and joy to be a member of L'Abri Fellowship. (CW, 5:167)

Rather than being hostile to his friendship with Schaeffer, as a very small vocal minority in America was, Rookmaaker's Calvinist friends and colleagues in Holland by and large were ambivalent. Rookmaaker himself perplexed them enough. Whether it was his nonreligious upbringing, the influence of the American Schaeffer, his particular personality traits, his sense of mission, or a combination of the above, he did not conform to their expectations of a conventional Dutch professor.

The journalistic spirit of Abraham Kuyper lived on in Rookmaaker. Hans was a born activist and communicator, two things academics rarely are. Before both his professorship and popularity abroad, he traveled around the Netherlands, glad to give talks and lectures to student groups, in churches, or at other special events. He enthusiastically and creatively conveyed his expertise in art history and/or African-American music combined with his religious convictions and outlook to captivated audiences. Some felt this activity came close to self-promotion and was unbecoming for a serious scholar. Money was not the motivation because he received little honoraria from these efforts. More to the point was the frequent absence from the Reformed mind-set of an appreciation for domestic missional engagement. Hans never forgot that there was virtually no attempt to take the opportunity to inform him of the faith at the Christian secondary school he had attended as a boy.

Rookmaaker's blending of his friendships with his work and with a sense of mission was as disconcerting for some as it was inspiring for others. Few handled better both of these possible feelings than Hans's exact contemporary, C.A. (Bert) van Swigchem, a friend and colleague of long standing. Van

Swigchem was much more of an insider in Calvinist circles than Hans was. Academically he had begun his career as a historian and later transitioned to the study of architectural history. He had a position at the Free University many years before Hans did and understood perhaps better than anyone else how a department of art history might be introduced there. In fact, in some respects his work was so significant in getting the department underway that he probably deserves to be called the co-founder of it, as he was there from its inception in 1964/1965, standing shoulder to shoulder with Hans.

Van Swigchem and Rookmaaker respected each other's views, whether they agreed or not. This translated into something that is rarely found: a frank relationship that was equally warmhearted. In a letter to van Swigchem dated April 6, 1961, well before they were colleagues, Hans wrote to say how much he appreciated van Swigchem's response to the book he had just written (*Kunst en Amusemusement/Art and Entertainment*, 1962). Not everything he read in the letter was to his liking, but the warmth of appreciation for the care with which van Swigchem had engaged with his work was evident. An exchange of honest thoughts, exhibited here, shows in hindsight that they both bore exceptional qualities of character to work realistically and effectively with each other later on. Hans reflected the security of their association when he wrote:

Dear Bert,
Thank you for your letter. I appreciate that you tell me what is on your heart.

I did not know at first what to do with your critique. You ask for a completely different book: How To Look At Art. I will do that later.

[First] I do not think that you read the times right. Your objections are not relevant in my experience. . . . There is a crisis and there are signs that want to be solved by a more direct Christian way of living.

[Second] You suggest that I do not have a good feeling for the Reformed public. That is why I wanted you to read it—to make it better and more relevant [there].

. . . You do not really say a lot about the text regarding my analysis of modern art and contemporary culture. Do I take this positively or negatively? Do you [also] mean I am not allowed to speak of The Apocalypse? I believe only in this way can one see clearly into the situation.

. . . Your letter has stimulated me to review the whole process, and I am grateful. I can accept your critique because on a deeper level we agree. . . .

Again thanks.

Hans

Van Swigchem admired Rookmaaker for his many initiatives and extensive professional and personal network of contacts. Hans was on excellent terms with the art-historical establishment in the Netherlands. That made life easier for both of them. When their department resources were minimal, their students were welcomed without a word to use the library of the University of Amsterdam and elsewhere. Hans brought repute to the new art history department through his research. Van Swigchem appreciated not only how strategic it had been for Hans to write his dissertation in English, but how rare it was for a Dutch dissertation ever to find its way into a new paperback edition as had been the case with *Synthetist Art Theories* (published as *Gauguin and Nineteenth-Century Art Theory* in 1972). When they did not have enough students to begin with, Rookmaaker created a museum assistant's certificate program that did not require prerequisites. The enthusiastic response filled classes and proved to be a recruiting ground for more students later. In their team effort, van Swigchem seems to have been a catalyst for other students to move over from history to study art and architectural history. Through their shared ideals and ideas they formed a special professional partnership that created a good working environment as staff were added to the department.

Maintaining this kind of balance was not easy. Although Hans may have felt disappointed that his colleague whom he admired was not interested in L'Abri Fellowship, van Swigchem was undoubtedly right not to get involved and convolute their relationship further. The distance between them probably made for a better friendship. Van Swigchem could more readily interpret needs of students coming out of typically Calvinist homes. He could also better see gaps in the day-to-day administration of a department that Hans overlooked as he became increasingly committed to activities abroad. Tensions arise in all close working relationships. Van Swigchem gave Rookmaaker the credit for their good relationship, but one suspects his own modesty and patience contributed a considerable amount to it as well.

No other friend had a better grasp of Hans's diverse networks in the Netherlands, Great Britain, the USA, and Canada than the American-born Dutchman and aesthetician Calvin Seerveld. They met in the 1950s, when Seerveld was in Europe pursuing graduate research in aesthetics in Italy, Switzerland, and the Netherlands.

The vague beginning of their relationship is belied by its uniqueness in the constellation of Hans's friendships. Seerveld cannot remember exactly when they met. He recollects with clarity, however, the impact it made on him as a young foreigner and scholar attending his initial meeting of the Association of Reformational Philosophy in Holland. These meetings, which Hans faithfully went to virtually each year, usually met at the famous American Hotel located in the heart of Amsterdam. Seerveld vividly remembers the night he flung open the door of the grand ballroom, eager to enter the gathering. A huge, dense cloud of smoke, hovering several yards above the heads of the crowd seated in the high-ceilinged room, hit him! Before the evening finished, he was also struck by the amazing mélange of people who were there—not just scholars and teachers but also ordinary church people with a concern for good and godly thinking and education. Rookmaaker could have been there. Seerveld could well have met him at such a meeting.

Seerveld remembers that early on while he was a poor graduate student living with, and almost a dependent of, his wife's family in The Hague, Hans introduced him to Henk Krijger, a painter with whom he eventually became a much closer friend. If Seerveld came to a major rescue job in defending the acceptance of Rookmaaker's dissertation in 1959, Hans in 1958 at least had come to Seerveld's aid in a minor way by being the first person ("the friendly questioner") out of four to begin the interrogation for the defense of Seerveld's dissertation in comparative literature and philosophy at the Free University. It was probably this history that made Hans bold enough to ask Seerveld to help him.

At Seerveld's oral examination, Hans's appreciation for jazz found an unusual opportunity for application. Although Rookmaaker was barely literate at that time on Benedetto Croce (1866–1952), the subject of the thesis, he managed to improvise and elaborate his questioning extensively for considerably longer than required, in order to give more time for the arrival of the next interrogator, K.J. Popma (1903–1986), a renowned Calvinist philosopher, classicist, and novelist who was nowhere in sight! As Hans was looking around longing to wind up his questioning, to everyone's relief the erudite and somewhat eccentric Popma appeared. The absentminded professor had taken a train to the wrong destination, but now he was there and all could proceed accordingly.

Rookmaaker and Seerveld became much closer during the course of Hans's first extensive trip to North America in 1961. At that time Seerveld was teaching at Trinity Christian College, a small undergraduate institution coming out of the Reformed tradition, located in Palos Heights, a suburb of Chicago. Hans stayed at Seerveld's home for a week in October of that year and bached it with him while Cal's wife was away visiting her relatives in the Netherlands.

Sharing improvised meals and driving around the Chicago area together to visit various colleges and art collections gave them ample opportunity for expansive conversation for which they previously had not had the opportunity. Without Seerveld as navigator and chauffeur, Rookmaaker may never have made it to his cherished visits to both Mahalia Jackson's church and to her home. The enormous collection of tapes and records of the Chicago-jazz expert John Steiner dazzled them both. Another evening they took off to hear the powerful trumpet playing of Bob Schoffner in a Chicago club. Today all of this seems innocent and natural for two professors of art theory and art/music history to be doing with their time. But in 1961 these were unusual activities for those teaching or giving lectures at evangelical or Reformed Christian colleges. The natural entrée Hans had into African-American circles also shows the breadth of his personal relationships, not merely the breadth of his personal interests.

The bonds of friendship were definitely deepened between Rookmaaker and Seerveld through their time together in Chicago. They shared a strong sense of calling for the cause of the Christian faith in their academic disciplines. Rookmaaker trusted Seerveld as a person he could confidently and confidentially share his professional aspirations with and seek honest help from. In the midst of his extended season of restlessness after returning from his trip to North America, Hans asked for Seerveld's advice. In straightforward language Seerveld exhorted him to stay at Leiden until something could open up at the Free University. The Free, in his opinion, was the best place for Hans to make an impact. Taking a position at a second-tier secular university or a Christian college in the USA was far less strategic in terms of long-range and lasting influence. Looking at all of this afterward and its seemingly self-evident nature, it is easy to lose sight of how sound Seerveld's counsel was not only for his friend's best interests but also for the promotion of Christian scholarship.

1. H.R.R.'s mother, Theodora Catharina Heitink (1890-1971), at age sixteen.

2. H.R.R.'s father, Henderik Roelof Rookmaaker, Senior (1887-1945) in the 1930s exuberantly bursting out in an *olé* during a flamenco.

3. A family photograph from 1924 shows Door trying her best to keep little Hansje in the picture despite the equatorial heat and glare of the sun.

4. H.R.R. and family in their residence in the Dutch Indies.

5. H.R.R., in naval uniform, stands beside his father.

6. This solemn snapshot of Riki betrays a realistic awareness of life.

7. Captain J.P.A. Mekkes (1897–1987), whom Hans met in 1943, became one of the most influential and faithful friends of his life.

8. On Wednesday, June 1, 1949, Hans and Anky were married in a civil ceremony, attended only by their immediate families, at the Town Hall of Amsterdam.

9. H.R.R. and Schaeffer during the 1960s and early 1970s exhibited a deep underlying affinity when they appeared together at L'Abri conferences held in North America and Europe.

10. H.R.R. and Francis Schaeffer during the Schaeffers' visit to Leiden around 1960.

11. H.R.R. in an art gallery.

12. H.R.R. with pipe.

While they both worked out of a thorough knowledge of Neo-Calvinist philosophy and endorsed an enormous amount in each other's vision and thinking, there were always significant running differences between them on aesthetic matters. Foremost was the dissimilarity of their approaches in understanding what constitutes the core meaning of the aesthetic sphere. Rookmaaker stood with the venerable tradition of "harmonious beauty" as key to the aesthetical dimension. For Seerveld the center resides in "allusiveness." The essence of art for the latter is its parabolic character and quality of multivalence. Intellectual differences never daunted their appreciation of each other. Iron sharpens iron. They had hoped to teach a course together at the Institute for Christian Studies in Toronto in the summer of 1977. Rookmaaker's death in March of that year prevented the plan they had long thought of from being fulfilled.

Schaeffer and Seerveld aside, it is amazing that Rookmaaker cultivated so many warmhearted and meaningful friendships in the Anglophone world. Other than professional contacts in the art-historical world, which were considerable, Hans's personal and cultural conditioning was a lot more tough-minded and generally sophisticated than most of the people he came to know in Britain and North America. Most Continentals of his ilk would have probably been expected to look on the attitudes he often encountered either as outdated or provincial if kindly disposed, or dismissed as ignorant if not so kindly disposed. One can only return to his perennial openness in not completely prejudging people or situations to appreciate the breadth and depth of the friendships in the English-speaking world that he developed.

Schaeffer was his vanguard, interestingly enough, in Britain. By the mid-1960s Schaeffer was speaking regularly at British universities, often in conjunction with the local Inter-Varsity Fellowship (IVF) Christian Union. There were also L'Abri conferences taking place. Rookmaaker was a great hit at these. It did not take long for the word to spread that he could intelligently and honestly critique a work of art. Eager artists filled with fear and trepidation at what they might hear from him brought their work for him to view at these gatherings.

The dainty pietism of much of British and American evangelicalism was antithetical to Rookmaaker's brand of realism. Younger artists and a number of progressive IVF staff workers in Britain knew that in him they had a friend and ally they could trust. They were ready for something more authentically engaged with their experience of life. They loved and respected him for his colorful and vigorous style in tackling and trying to understand the manifestations in Western culture that robbed people of their full humanness. The so-called stuffy British were the least reserved of his fans and affectionately dubbed him "Rooky."

The evangelical establishment on both sides of the Atlantic, however, was more wary of him. Inter-Varsity Press in the UK questioned him as to whether it was necessary or wise to use paintings of the nude to make his points in a book he was planning to write for them. They considered it a serious problem. It might be fine in the context of an art college but not proper at all for ordinary parishioners into whose hands it might fall, for the press intended to see that his book was distributed as widely as possible. Fortunately, it fell to the lot of the talented and diplomatic editor David Alexander to work with Hans to bring forth the book we know today as *Modern Art and the Death of a Culture* (nudes and all!)—probably the first true crossover book IVP ever published.

While Rookmaaker may have had a broad grin like the Cheshire cat when he smiled, he was not a domesticated animal but rather an untamed one that disturbed the insecure and empowered the semi-confident. He was deliberately provocative:

> You took Christian standards for granted. The young people said to you, 'Why do life [in] this or that way?' and you said, 'Never bother me with questions; just do it.' But they are intelligent young men and women. They have looked at the world and they have made up their own standards. You say we should fight pornography? Yes, we should fight pornography, but remember

it only came this far because we Christians were not there when we should have been there. Now the battle is lost and we can only clean up the battlefield. So do not say 'Wicked young people sleeping with each other,' but say 'Wicked Christians who did not explain well when the questions were being asked.'

Urging Christian people to wake up and shake off a couple of centuries of sleep was not an easy or appreciated task.

In 1966, after Rookmaaker's article "Letter to a Christian Artist" appeared in *Christianity Today*, he became embroiled in a running controversy with its editors as he tried to challenge them to think critically about the kind of art they were publishing in its pages. The case in point was in regard to reproductions of the work of a contemporary American artist with religious themes that Rookmaaker thought made *CT* look ridiculous in the eyes of outsiders and whom the editors defended as being fine work by a leading American artist. The issues and attitudes here were (and are) far more important than the names of those involved. Rookmaaker's frank response was more blunt than customary and startling:

> Even if [this artist] is a real Christian, [he] is not an artist that can be talked about seriously as an artist. If this is Christian art, it would mean that we Christians have no art, probably not even the mentality or will to have art at all. It would prove that Christianity is in principle not compatible with art . . . the Head of Christ is a complete failure and as subject matter—it is difficult as such—far above the possibilities of the artist. . . . The second one, the weeping woman, is again a complete failure—it did not even succeed in being sentimental . . . a young man making these would have a hard time getting entrance to any academy, and really not because people do not like Christian work or only accept modernist art. . . .
>
> I personally feel that either my own work—to promote the cause of Christian endeavour in the arts, both critically and creatively—is a hard necessity, meaning that it seems to be

much harder than I ever thought it would be, or my work is hopeless, and I better stop doing it. . . . I really mean it—that if this is Christian art, I should stop working for it, and if this is real art in the line of Rembrandt, I should never like to think of art anymore. You must believe me that this is a *cri de coeur*, as I am sure I am not alone. Those to whom I showed these works here in Holland all reacted as I do.

I am perfectly aware that things cannot be changed anymore. I am not asking you to publish this—you can if you wish to—but I simply had to write this to unburden my conscience and to warn you against experiments in this line. I am really sorry for your work, which has now been stained by it. I'm sure, without your realizing what was happening.

Sincerely Yours in Christ,
Hans Rookmaaker

Christianity Today's editors stereotypically declared that the artist in question had to be good because he graduated from "the leading art school in America" and his name was listed in *Who's Who in American Art*. The leadership at the publication suggested that people simply respond to works differently and they obviously had no desire to prolong a discussion on the topic of art. Rookmaaker tenaciously chewed on his art bone, coming back again and again to suggest that something very important was at stake that they should treat with utmost seriousness. In late January 1967 he wrote:

The strangeness of modern art is partly due to an attitude of protest against pictures like these and what they stand for. So if we defend them, our case must be strongly [grounded]. I feel the protest is right, but the antichristian direction it takes and the resulting absurdity is horrible. We Christians must search and work towards a new and fresh art, twentieth-century and biblical, without compromise or synthesis with worldly streams.

Hoping to meet you, and sincerely yours in the Lord,
Hans Rookmaaker

Church audiences who trashed modern art were stunned when he turned to them and said, "How can you say that modern art is ugly when you worship the Lord in a building painted like this?" The response Rookmaaker sought from evangelicals gradually came, somewhat more quickly in Great Britain than in North America. Rookmaaker's toughness did not merely take ideas seriously but people just as much, if not more seriously. He was not out to score intellectual points but to nurture relationships that could work for realistic change in the world, nothing too high-falutin. "Compare van Goyen with the work of Claude or any of the Italianate painters. They present a world you can never have. It is good to have dreams but if the quality of that dream is forced it will only lead to frustration. We must dream towards an attainable end."

Linette Martin tells of a student who complained on a beautiful day of not having a swimming pool nearby as Rookmaaker stood with him. Rookmaaker immediately retorted with not a little anger, "If you think like that you will never enjoy life! You will always be frustrated and you will never make the most of opportunities around you! There is so much to enjoy. If you think only of what isn't there, you'll never be happy!" Words like these were characteristic of a man who knew what it was like to reconstruct most of the dreams and desires of his life after a devastating war. His shock tactics were not meant to harm but to stir to life "the living dead" of our age.

Rooky was a breath of fresh air, or more precisely, a special aromatic air as he wafted his pipe while making gallant gestures to punctuate points when he spoke. For those with a real nose to smell, his aroma lingered with them long after in a life-giving way. Here was a real personality who could inspire others to think and could encourage them to dream attainable dreams they never dared think of before. He was remarkably transparent in his relationships. Although there was often rich reciprocity in his closest friendships, they brought him little worldly advantage. He simply knew how to be a friend who never ceased caring for his neighbor, even if he often expressed it pungently and provocatively.

SEVEN

PASSIONS

Hans Rookmaaker's words left unforgettable echoes in the ears and hearts of his hearers. His convictions were completely and creatively united with the manner of his expression. Beneath his ordinary appearance was a potent subterranean quality of controlled intensity that infiltrated his expression, giving it an implicit evocativeness. The discrepancy between the conventional packaging and the restrained force of feeling below the surface of his speech charged his communication with a tangy quality. Not all people were prepared for the robustness of his style. He could exclaim, for example, "All truth is relative," and send his devout listeners into shock until with impeccable timing he resuscitated them by supplying the predicate, "to Jesus Christ."

Rookmaaker displayed considerable personal professorial dignity, but academic aloofness played no part in his expressive style or the content of his work. The secret of Hans's ability to engage the imaginations of so many struggling with the issues of the arts, culture, and belief was that his own imagination was thoroughly engaged. His leading themes were not mere abstract ideas but passions that came from hard-won experience. His way of knowing was participatory. In his own life he integrated the intellectual, emotional, and volitional to a high degree and did not drive a wedge between the physical and spiritual realms.

Since the Enlightenment, formal education has focused almost exclusively on the cultivation of the intellect, neglecting the feelings and the will. Somehow Rookmaaker managed to educate his feelings commensurately so that they made a remarkable bridge between his ideas and his sense of action. His formative years in a non-Western culture and early and continuous exposure to jazz and other forms of African-American music were probably also influential in catapulting him away from being a predictable professor.

This could also have influenced his aptitude for a qualitative appreciation of history. History viewed in this way suggests that over the course of time human nature does not necessarily remain static. Not only do ideas and events change, but people also change. An important interlocutor for him on this subject was Jan Hendrik van den Berg, a learned historian of psychiatry who was especially cognizant of the cultural and historical rootedness of phenomenological psychology. His book *Metabletica of Leer der veranderingen: beginselen van een historische psychologie* (published in English in 1961 as *The Changing Nature of Man*) detailed with abundant historical specificity directions and intuitions toward which Hans's thinking was already heading. Hans was deeply immersed at the time in the rich, visual documentation for an understanding of subject matter in art being gathered by the Iconclass project in which he was involved at Leiden. Van den Berg did not create his outlook but seems to have confirmed his own understanding of the cultural and historical embeddedness of thought. Personal correspondence in 1961 and 1962 confirms their mutual appreciation of each other's work, although van den Berg's perspective was more broadly humanistic rather than specifically Christian.

Both van den Berg and Rookmaaker were ahead of their times in their critique of modernity. In *Metabletica*, van den Berg described the changing relation between adults and children over the centuries in the West that has led to an increasingly prolonged infantilization and adolescence, delaying the taking on of adult responsibilities by young people. Van den Berg observed a web of attitudes and events surrounding childhood synchronically rather than simply tracing a discrete line of explicit exposition on childhood diachronically. Simply put, childhood had been extended since the Renaissance. It was not possible to read some kind of law of uniformity regarding the rearing of children back into history. There were qualitative differences and changes. This made an impact on contemporary practices of parenting and education and many other areas of life that most people never reflected on and took completely for granted. Hans immediately could see the application of this approach to other spheres. Culture surrounded art, and art also was a lens through which to view culture and philosophical ideas.

Van den Berg liked the way Hans linked art with the art of living, but he also was academically savvy enough to know that specialists in art history were not apt to agree with Hans's approach. He found it refreshing that Hans had the courage to articulate his convictions with clear language more than he felt he himself did.

This qualitative approach to history meant that art was not simply an illustration of the past. Although art was independently justified, it was not autonomous and offered a means to interpret the culture and philosophical belief systems of which it was a part. Rookmaaker was not particularly interested in systematic or philosophical theology. He was a serious lay reader of the Bible with a perspective more sympathetic to biblical theology. The thematic unity of the biblical writings fascinated him and exhibited for him not merely the cleverness of human writers but the Authorship of God, who continued to love, live, and work in history. At times to the point of polemicizing, Rookmaaker maintained that the authentic worldview underlying seventeenth-century Dutch art was a biblical one consistent with Scripture. In a strict sense he did not do theology through art; that is, he did not exegete art primarily for theological meaning. But he also did not do theology of the arts as was and is so fashionable; that is, he did not talk about art from the perspective of theological conceptions and generalizations of an abstract nature.

He was geared to understanding the meaning embedded in the works of art themselves rather than interpolating theology into the arts. Rookmaaker was, however, an important precursor of the "theology through art" approach because he sought cultural, philosophical, and to some degree biblical insight through individual, concrete works of art rather than taking works of art as a pretext to explain ideas. (This is explained further in Chapter 8.)

Rookmaaker was also a precursor of the now more widely spread understanding of art monuments as historical documents that can supplement the textual record and bring to light new insights of times past that ordinarily might be overlooked without their consideration. Already in the 1950s as an art critic he could write:

> Then there is the strange and very beautiful crucifix from Brunswijk, carved a century or so later during the mid-twelfth century by Master Imerwald. Indeed, one aspect of the appeal of these sculptures is that they are amongst the earliest examples (still) in circulation. One of the oldest figures of the Madonna we know originates from a church in Essen. It is a wooden sculpture covered in gold leaf and dates back to the tenth century. It is important and interesting both for art his-

torians and church historians, even though most of us will not find it particularly attractive. (*CW*, 1:234)

No examination of Rookmaaker's view of history can omit the formative and substantial influence on him of the thought and writings of Guillaume Groen van Prinsterer (1801–1876), archivist and historian to the Dutch monarch. As a deeply believing man, Groen sought to articulate and evaluate underlying assumptions influencing events by the light cast on them by Scripture. Hans found affinity with this approach and seems naturally to have come to a similar practice during the process of his conversion.

He especially valued two published works by the royal historian. The first, a handbook of Dutch history (*Handboek der Vaderlandse Geschiedenis*, 1846), Hans declared to be "one of the most wonderful books on history that I have ever read" (*CW*, 6:175). On the basis of the documents he was working with, Groen felt compelled in this book to rewrite the history of Holland from a Calvinist, Christian perspective. In it he took issue with a secularist interpretation promulgated by Enlightenment writers that denigrated the Protestant influence of the House of Orange on the creation of the Dutch republic. This work became a textbook in schools and established a new way of looking at the origin of the nation that valued its Reformation heritage. The second work, *Ongeloof en Revolutie* (*Unbelief and Revolution*), was delivered originally as a series of lectures in 1847 on the topic of the French Revolution. Hans felt that Groen's exposition of the implications of the antithetical principles animating the Reformation and the French Revolution read not only as history but also as prophecy.

Rookmaaker was passionate about this kind of history that stepped beyond detachment into life. It had a ring of reality to it that abided with him. Groen, on the basis of his historical study, called for action, even though he considered himself more of a theorist. The unbelief that drove the French Revolution, expunging God from every sphere of society and the state, was still alive and causing consequences that did not lead to freedom but to new forms of bondage. Presciently, for example, Groen predicted the disruptiveness and destructiveness that the unfettered expansion of a revolutionary drive for unlimited individual rights would have upon an understanding of the nature of justice. His distinctly antirevolutionary stance led the way for his most famous follower, Abraham Kuyper, a man of action, to translate historical analysis into a popularly based political party, supported by grassroots lay citizens in the Reformed tradition who had felt disenfranchised prior to that time. In 1879, three years after the death of Groen van Prinsterer, the Anti-Revolutionary Party (ARP) was formed under Kuyper's leadership to bring a practical application of belief into political, social, and cultural life in the Netherlands.

In "A Dutch Christian View of Philosophy," Rookmaaker identified himself wholeheartedly as a student of Groen and Kuyper and paid tribute to their vision and achievement:

> [T]hey understood that Christianity is not just religion, Christianity is not just the church, Christianity is not just a good feeling in your heart because you are saved and going to heaven but Christianity is all of life and it is the covenant. We walk with God and he is taking care of his people and we should walk in his ways and look at the world with an open Bible and use the key that the Bible provides for us to understand the world, everything, not just religion but everything. And they talked about this and they founded a political party. This party was called the Anti-Revolutionary Party, which meant that they were anti the spirit of the French Revolution, which is the Enlightenment, which is autonomous human being, which I always talk about because I too am a pupil of Groen. (CW, 6:176)

Biblical and historical understanding intricately intertwined with Hans's passion for freedom, another continuous theme in his life and works. He would shake his head and express with his entire body a heaviness and disappointment at the lack of freedom he found in the church and among Christians. He ached in befuddlement and frustration at the contradiction of his believing brothers and sisters in this area as he heard preaching that proclaimed that Christ sets people free, but saw a legalism that inhibited believers and held them back from being preserving salt and purifying light in their society. Knowing there can be no genuine creativity and authentic art without freedom, he grieved visibly for young Christian artists experiencing this restrictive environment.

Freedom, true intellectual and spiritual liberation, was the capstone of his own conversion. How would any Christian want to forfeit it? He had come to experience this freedom while in physical captivity in a Nazi POW camp. This freedom was embedded entirely in an understanding of the living reality of Jesus Christ and his servant Paul's exposition of this truth. Freedom captivated Rookmaaker's imagination and set him on a creatively constructive way of life. Authentic freedom, as he knew it, means to be able to develop as a human creature in accordance with reality. We see how basic and biblical this understanding was for him: "I simply cannot accept—on the contrary, it strikes me as unscriptural—that when a person becomes a Christian she or he must be inhibited and lose their freedom. No, the Christian's portion is life—instead of death and freedom, being truly human"(*CW*, 3:336).

His feeling for freedom contrasted with legalism as much as it did with a prevalent permissiveness without rules or norms that contemporary culture promoted. The latter led to libertinism rather than true liberty, creating ever greater tyranny and despair. He stated over and over again in many variations that Christ died not to make us Christian but to make us human. Being fully human meant being fully free.

Hans could be outspoken, but rarely was he ready to call down a judgmental opinion on others or for that matter on himself. David Muir, a British professional storyteller, remembers one occasion when Rookmaaker was asked if it was inconsistent to be a Christian and a smoker. Hans immediately pulled his pipe out of his pocket and put it in his mouth as he contemplated his answer. His reply (as Muir remembers) was, "God has a distinct record of accepting burnt offerings from those who really loved and feared him, and I am certainly one. If there perchance comes a whiff of tobacco from any light I give out, well, let's leave God to his judgments and us to our obedience to his calling of and for us."

Hans's humanity may have been perplexing to the less alive. For believing artists, bursting with life, he was a revelation. At the beginning of his artistic journey, Muir knew this to be true and calls him today "a man who really knew what it is to walk that straight and narrow way and while doing so giving us a great example of how to walk in moral and aesthetic freedom and enjoy it at the same time."

At the heart of who Hans was, was a passion for beauty. As a theme in his works, it is ubiquitous. Harmonious beauty stands for him at the center of the aesthetical sphere and is woven into the fabric of all of creation. Yet beauty alone did not define art for him. His love of beauty did not make him a reverent devotee of beauty as such or a prissy aesthete. He was vehemently against aestheticism, an attitude that insists that beauty is the most important aspect in art and/or life and to which everything should be subservient. He looked for loveliness that goes unnoticed in the ordinary surrounding us everyday. The writer and editor Sharon Gallagher has a vivid recollection of being exhorted by Hans during a visit by him to Berkeley, California, in 1972 to walk home each day by a different route so that she could see afresh the beauty that surrounded her all of the time. A simple suggestion became an avenue to enhanced living for her that she has bid others try.

Seventeenth-century Dutch art was a celebration of the beauty of the ordinary in common life and served as an example par excellence of everyday treasures. In many ways it epitomized the quintessence of Rookmaaker's aesthetic values. Some have thought his dedicated appreciation of it captivated him to a degree that diminished his ability to regard, even understand, the art of other times, especially the modern period. This, however, would be a serious misreading both of his spirit and his works, which copiously show his positive engagement with art of all periods and also with some non-Western art.

This is not to deny that he had a special attachment to the art of the Golden Age. He did. And it came naturally and straight out of his spiritual kinship with the tradition of Groen van Prinsterer and Abraham Kuyper.

Rookmaaker, though a student and admirer of Kuyper, was not an uncritical recipient of everything the latter said, especially his pronouncements on art in his Stone Lectures (1898). But he agreed when his fellow Dutchman and distinguished modern pioneer of the integration of learning and life stated the influence of Calvinism on Dutch art at its most glorious effulgence:

. . . under the auspices of Calvinism, the art of painting, prophetic of democratic life of later times, was the first to proclaim the people's maturity. . . . [N]on-churchly life was also possessed of high importance and of an all-sided art-motive. Having been overshadowed for many centuries by class-distinctions, the common life of man came out of its hiding-place like a new world, in all its sober reality . . . the idea of election by free grace has contributed not a little toward interesting art in the hidden importance of what was small and insignificant. If a common man, to whom the world pays no special attention, is valued and even chosen by God as one of His elect, this must lead the artist also to find a motive for his artistic studies in what is common and of everyday occurrence, to pay attention to the emotions and the issues of the human heart in it. . . . Thus far the artist had only traced upon his canvas the idealized figures of prophets and apostles, of saints and priests; now, however, when he saw how God had chosen the porter and the wage-earner for Himself, he found interest not only in the head, the figure and the entire personality of the man of the people, but began to reproduce the human expression of every rank and station.

The towering Protestant visual interpreter of the Bible, Rembrandt van Rijn, managed to bring home the prophets and apostles to the world of seventeenth-century common life and to render an encyclopedic cast of everyday characters as participants in holy history. In his preoccupation with biblical subjects, Rembrandt was unusual as the trend of his century was more toward an exquisite naturalism represented through landscape, portraiture, genre interiors, and still lifes rather than biblical subjects. Furthermore, superb artists such as Jan van Goyen, Jan Steen, Johannes Vermeer, amongst Rookmaaker's favorite artists, were Roman Catholic. Confessional status was not the issue. Calvinism in a deep and rich way, Kuyper and Rookmaaker believed, had pervaded the whole culture in Holland in the seventeenth century, so that everyone was the recipient of its liberating benefits whether they were technically Catholic or Protestant. Life had been qualitatively and immensely enriched for everyone. Rookmaaker pointed out particular ways in which he thought this was so:

> Jan van Goyen made us see the particular beauty and the characteristics of the structure of our great rivers, Paulus Potter (and many others) depicted the Dutch cattle, Van Ostade helped us to better appreciate the colourful country life, and so on. Especially the painters of later times—since the fifteenth century—have taught us to see (as a result of the nature of their art). Did Heda not show us the beauty of a glass which reflects light, did Kalff not open our eyes to the amazing reflections of light on silver? The paintings of our seventeenth century are, each in their own way, 'iconic' songs about the beauty of God's creation, poems about the joy of this earthly

life—very sober and realistic, and without denying the effects of sin and the fall. (*CW*, 4:228)

Rookmaaker was no aesthete, but he was wonderfully discriminating, looking ardently for beauty in the small and inconsequential. As he traveled, he loved villages and out-of-the-way places, not just big cities and glitzy galleries. In Switzerland and Austria the aesthetic brought forward by seventeenth-century Dutch art allowed him to see the wise use of land in the integration of farm buildings within the landscape in a way that beautified it and added charm to it. But in the United States and Canada, it led him to observe a more appropriative and instrumental use of land that often led to the scarring and ugliness of the landscape, though it was as inherently beautiful as anything in Europe. Nothing was generally added that graced it. Of course, he was aware that some of the same values he saw written in the landscape of North America were also coming to Europe.

The art of seventeenth-century Holland gave Rookmaaker a place to stand aesthetically parallel to his firm footing philosophically in the tradition of Calvinist thought. Far from restricting him, this aesthetic gave him enormous scope. A few of the things it helped him love were: clarity, modesty, restraint, decorum, splendor without ostentation, simplicity without bareness, humanity, warmth, expressiveness without emotionalism, playfulness, humor, elegance, faithfulness to nature without slavish realism, and charm. He admired the minimalist elegance of much of modern art, especially in its application to contemporary design. His sensibilities had no trouble leaping from the pristine vast spaces of whitewashed church interiors by Pieter Saenredam (1597–1665) to the bare essentialism in the geometrical abstract style of Piet Mondrian (1872–1944).

Linked to Hans's fervent attachment to beauty was his appreciation and high view of women. He may well have been living in another universe, certainly another age, in how he expressed this in his comportment. In his day and today the cold trivialization of sex and the absence of transcendence in most people's lives makes it difficult to describe the qualitative complexity of his expression of eros, but it was there and very real.

Rookmaaker was no ladies' man, but he loved women—and not just beautiful women. Despite his unexceptional exterior, through his restrained intensity he had a powerful effect on women because he was truly both interesting to them and interested in them, in their ideas and sensibilities. He could equally irk and run off young women who fawned and were sentimental and thought creating candlelight settings was the essence of charm. He would literally turn on the highest-powered light that he could find when this happened! There were nudges and winks on occasion when he took interest in a young woman as he shepherded her around an art museum, but his interest did not translate into transgression. He was well aware of the wealth of experience he shared with his wife, Anky, a treasure never worth losing. He also supported her in a career of philanthropy that did not take off until she was in her fifties, and he was justifiably proud of her achievements. He knew that his strength and credibility in communicating came from commitments he had made, particularly in marriage.

He was neither romantic nor puritanical. Agape and eros were not pitted against each other in his personality but were embraced in a way rare for our times. In this way he lived like Bach, who was not a man to go about town womanizing, but was not frightened at weaving sexuality into the spiritual meaning of his cantatas in a way that is still surprising if one really reflects on the content of his texts. Two of Hans's favourite Bach cantatas exemplify an eroticism that is foreign to our own times but was as natural a way of being for Hans as it was for Bach.

In the first, "O Everlasting Fire, O Source of Love" ("O ewiges Feuer, O Ursprung der Liebe," BWV 34), a cantata Bach had written for the wedding of a pastor, he had little trouble later seamlessly recycling it with minimal changes for Pentecost, remembering the coming down of the Holy Spirit in tongues of fire on his bride, the church, after Jesus' ascension. The second, "Wake, Arise, the Voices Call Us" (*"Wachet auf, ruft uns die Stimme*," BWV 140), a cantata for the last Sunday in the calendar of the Christian year before Advent, speaks of a wedding. Its biblical anchoring in the parable of the ten virgins (Matthew 25:1–13) compresses eschatological preparedness with the expectant intimacy of a bridegroom about to consummate his marriage. The duet aria sung by the soprano and basso is a joyous celebration of bliss in union even as it is an allusion to words in the Song of Solomon (2:16; 6:3):

> *Soprano (Bride/Soul):* My friend is mine. *Basso (Bridegroom/ Jesus):* And I am thine. *Both in union:* Let love bring no division. *Both at the same time, but not in unison: Soprano (Bride/Soul):* I will with thee on heaven's roses pasture. *Basso (Bridegroom/Jesus):* Thou shalt with me on heaven's roses pasture. Where pleasure in fullness, where joy will abound.

In the 1970s the siege mentality of pious evangelicals was evident in the area of sexual mores, even as a proactive engagement on the way to social justice was often sadly lacking. Between the secular proponents of sexual promiscuousness and the backlash from pulpits propounding all-encompassing agape at the expense of eros, Rookmaaker may not have stood entirely alone, but he was isolated and threatening in his own way in this area, particularly to some insecure British types consumed with concern about "the permissive society." Sexuality was not a topic he spoke on explicitly. But it was one he knew a great deal about, as it was related to the subject matter of much of the art he dealt with. All those nudes he talked about made some nervous. Because he could exegete through art the qualitative changing nature of sexual relations over the centuries, he was able to understand the degradation he found in his own day. But it also helped him handle it healthily with hope, suggesting a better, more biblical way rather than reactive fear. He modeled something valuable in this area for the sexually indulgent as much as for the sexually judgmental.

Beauty and love in the widest and deepest way went together for Hans. He said:

> To speak of a beautiful act is thus to my mind not a metaphorical use of terms. Because the act was in obedience to the Second great Commandment, to love our neighbor as ourselves, it could also be beautiful, in the sphere that for want of a better word we refer to as the aesthetic.
>
> Loveliness is something we should seek, says the Lord. That speaks for itself: it is inappropriate for believers who desire to love their neighbours and to be salting salt to go through life snarling and growling! . . . Although in reality matters are sometimes uncannily tangled up in a hopeless knot of sin and wretchedness and goodness and beauty, it is remarkable to see how love can ennoble someone's face, so that someone who is not very attractive by nature can still be regarded as very beautiful, as having a kind of beauty that is not based directly on the harmonious proportion of shapes but that is all the same striking. On the other hand we can sometimes see very beautiful women whose beauty is hard and pitiless, cruel in sensuality—think of many photos of film stars and of women in advertisements. One is confronted often enough with this sort of "ugly beauty." (CW, 3:101)

Hans would probably not have been an easy personality to define in any age, but he was especially not so in one that relegated matters of meaning to a reductive understanding of history and eschewed the Bible on the basis of a prejudicial cultural reception of it rather than a firsthand reading of its text. It is only possible to intimate that he reflected and embodied, not only with his words but also with his entire being, a rejection of what he considered to be an intellectually and spiritually impoverished culture and a frequently effete expression of Christian faith within it. His passion for modern art was positive and central to his work, not because he agreed with the message of meaning-lessness and absurdity in much of it, but because it gave an accurate reading of the times that few were willing to face, whether they called themselves Christian or not.

Rookmaaker was an exceptionally integrated person, full of contrasts, polarities, and tensions. He was earthy and sensuous, but also spiritually minded and sober; rough-hewn and refined; fierce but gentle; courteous, yet capable of being rude. At times it was difficult to know whether he was being playful or profoundly serious. He would lead his hearers to anticipate being amused and then suddenly, when they started to laugh, say gravely, "You should not laugh, you should weep!" He was no pietist, but he was a man of deep piety and sincerity.

His passions were many—many more than have been suggested here. His aesthetics took deep root in everyday reality. He imbibed the fullness of life and shared it to the utmost. He certainly identified with Bach's little ditty: "On land, on sea, at home, abroad, I smoke my pipe and worship God!"

EIGHT

LEGACY

The last years of Hans Rookmaaker's life were filled with incessant activity as he met his commitments at home and traveled extensively abroad. Then in a mere moment, at the height of his influence and impact, all was suspended in an instant. At an unsuspected hour on a day beginning to bud into spring in March 1977 his earthly life was over.

In their shock and sorrow Hans's family was inspired to choose a profoundly appropriate text from one of his favorite books of the Bible, Revelation, to announce his death. The passage reads:

"Blessed are the dead who die in the Lord from now on."
"Blessed indeed," says the Spirit, "that they may rest from

their labors, for their deeds follow them." (Revelation 14:13b, English Standard Version)

In fifty-five years (exactly the same number of years allotted to his spiritual ancestor John Calvin), Rookmaaker's work in this world was completed. The legacy of his labor has followed; and in many ways it is only getting underway more than twenty-five years after his death. His work continues not only to benefit believers of all denominational stripes who are active in the arts but also to honor the Calvinist tradition with which he identified himself.

Ordinarily scholars influence other scholars in their field through their research and writings. But the reach of Rookmaaker's impact on others expands well beyond academic art-historical circles, through both his writings and personal contacts, to include artists and musicians, poets and publishers, filmmakers and philosophers, and even a few theologians and educators in other areas. While the exceptional diversity of his impact reflects Rookmaaker's many interests, it also refracts a personality of complexity and a character not easily classifiable by convenient categories, sacred or secular. Rookmaaker did not have star attraction, as popularly understood; but he did have appeal for individuals from a wide spectrum of society. He was under no illusion about his capacity to captivate everyone he encountered. But he was aware that there were some few with whom he truly could communicate and help.

Those who possessed a desire or a capacity to nurture their imaginations toward goodness were drawn to him like bees to honey when they read his books or heard him speak. He might not have articulated his basic aim in these terms, but this was what he was after, and this accounts for the amazing diversity of individuals from different nationalities he managed to interest, his appeal across disciplines and professions, his credibility with women as well as men, and his persuasiveness with a younger generation coming along today.

For those who connected with him, he was more than a masterful teacher—he was an inspirer. He had phenomenal power to motivate. British artist and art educator Peter Smith writes: "It is no secret that, like many others, I came across Rookmaaker at a crucial time in my life. The list of those who are still active in the fields of the Arts in the broadest sense, let alone other disciplines, who would admit to some kind of debt to Rookmaaker is . . . long. Rookmaaker's biblical and Reformational thinking about the Arts re-located many of us in a fuller and richer world with the freedom and responsibility to serve Christ beyond the confines of Pietism."

"Hans Rookmaaker not only talked about history. He made history." That is the estimation of the American art historian Rachel Smith (no relation to Peter Smith), who is too young to have known Rookmaaker personally but who discovered his writings as an undergraduate before embarking on her academic career. The history she refers to is the conversion of attitude toward the arts that he was so significantly instrumental in causing among conservative Protestants, a change that opened the way for someone like herself, coming from a Reformed church background, to take up the arts with impunity and embrace them with joy as some of God's greatest gifts to humanity.

The change Rookmaaker helped so notably to create did not come dramatically or through any systematic agenda that he promulgated, but rather softly and steadily, through a weaving of his biblical vision and voice with his personal relationships as he pursued his profession as an art historian and his calling as a Christian to integrate his faith with his learning.

While Rookmaaker's influence has developed slowly and subtly over the course of time through those on whom he has left his mark, the actual pace of his life in his last decade was very fast even by today's electronically driven standards for speed, and this contributed to his astounding impact on people. The qualitative contribution he made to the lives of so many individuals and organizations during those years represents a staggering emotional and spiritual investment that is still paying artistic and scholarly dividends.

From the late 1960s until his death, Rookmaaker gave massive energy to mentoring a whole host of people. Not all of them were his official students. Single-mindedly he directed his academic career in the service of his calling in a way that went beyond narrowly defined notions of professorial duty and frequently ran counter to administrative expectations at his university. He may be admired for this; he may also be criticized for this. It may have caused him at times to neglect some of his official students.

Rookmaaker's relationship with Graham Birtwistle, one of his first foreign-born graduate students and today an associate professor in modern art at the Free University of Amsterdam, contains many aspects of the complexities of Hans's last years as well as his authenticity of spirit in encountering the issues facing his students and dedication in sustaining personal relationships.

By the time Birtwistle heard of the name Hans Rookmaaker, "the Flying Dutchman" (a name given to him by Linette Martin) was just beginning to flit from the Netherlands back and forth to Great Britain routinely. In 1961 Rookmaaker had taken his first grand tour of North America, but the days of his comings and goings to North America regularly were still ahead of him. Birtwistle first got wind of the peripatetic professor, both by reputation of his personal appearances in the UK and by his scholarly repute, as he was transitioning from being a student in art history and English literature at Manchester University to lecturing in art history at Leicester Polytechnic.

An intellectual ride with Rookmaaker was always interesting. As with so many others, it began with a bumpy start for Birtwistle. While Birtwistle was a believer when he met his future mentor, almost by accident, on a visit to L'Abri Fellowship in Switzerland, he was not prepared to concede many of his own deeply held personal preferences in art, which tended toward a subjective Romanticism, or to assess the intellectual assumptions of his educational formation critically in light of his Christian beliefs. Rookmaaker listened to him and challenged him intellectually and spiritually on these fronts in a way that Birtwistle had never known before from his religious upbringing and never experienced in his formation afterward.

The seriousness with which he was taken and the cogency of Rookmaaker's thinking contributed to his reassessment of his previous ideas. So much so that he decided to go to the Netherlands, learn Dutch, and study for a doctorate in art history with Rookmaaker, a decision that eventually led to his current appointment.

So the story of Birtwistle is not without its twists and turns. His initial reaction to Rookmaaker represents a pattern. Many, on first engaging Rookmaaker's thinking, especially his utterances on modern art, did and do dismiss him and his ideas summarily. One often hears thoughtful people, many of whom are practicing artists, reject his work because they perceive that he did not understand modern art, that he hated it and wanted only to see contemporary art that looked like it was made for, if not in, the seventeenth century. In their view, abstraction was anathema for him. Rookmaaker's provocative style and unwillingness to bow to the fashionable trends of the times only made him all the more susceptible to bracketing his views and considering him reactive and out of touch rather than seeing him as offering a broader and deeper, boldly sophisticated critique. Although it is understandable how some have stayed at this stage of engagement with Rookmaaker's thought, it is unfortunate that they have missed his philosophical criticism of modernity and confused it with a dismissal and damnation of modern art.

For the man who formed the foundations of his thinking in the furnace of World War II, the stakes were high. Ideas reflected in modern art were not just neutral or nice, coincidental concepts. They were loaded with philosophical presuppositions as to the meaning of reality. When art institutions went out of their way to evangelize, one might say, for the cause of modern art, there was more happening than just making the general public aware of new art. In Rookmaaker's judgment, they were preaching and making propaganda for a view of reality totally antithetical to the acknowledgement of a creational order given by a loving and living Creator. It was "[r]eality . . . experienced as an alien power, irrational, strange, imprisoning humankind with its laws. . . . They experience their own lives as meaningless accidents and feel they have been thrown into a sick reality" (CW, 1:321).

Rookmaaker had come near to walking down the same road himself in the chaos of war until he became convinced of a richer and deeper way of experiencing life in Christian freedom. He longed for others to know such fullness of life. He understood the temptation of this route; and in many ways he had tremendous compassion for those captivated by their alienation and seduced by modern art as a surrogate religion. Rookmaaker took modern art with absolute seriousness. He decried Christians who dismissed it and ignored it. For him, it was a key indicator of the condition of the times. He saw value and a certain achievement in Picasso's rejection of Enlightenment thinking, but he was not beguiled by the creed the artist went on to promote in its place. He also could appreciate modern art's breaking down the dogma of naturalism espoused by much nineteenth-century academic art that in its own way distorted reality as much as any art of the twentieth century.

Rather than a specific style or particular spiritual pedigree, Rookmaaker was looking for evidence of the affirmation of our humanity situated in meaningful reality in contemporary art. His deep appreciation of the art of Georges Rouault's dark, yet redemptive vision is a case in point to disabuse those who believe that he never had any appreciation for the art of the modern era. He could acknowledge the beauty in an abstract painting by Jackson Pollock. But the arrogance of willfully trashing a world still filled with evidences of God's glory despite sin and evil incensed him. Still, he was aware that "[i]f modern art is sometimes oppressive and negative in direction, then we as believers [also] bear some of the responsibility" (*CW*, 4:370-371).

Graham Birtwistle, along with many others, learned that Rookmaaker was not an intransigent opponent of modern art but rather a critic with whom one could have a meaningful dialogue, one who could open up understanding on both sides of a conversation. Birtwistle was not sidelined into writing on some "safe" and approved area but dealt with art that Rookmaaker had little liking for or personal sympathy with, to say the least. His doctoral dissertation took up a reevaluation of COBRA (acronym for Copenhagen, Brussels, Amsterdam), a movement as well as a style of post-World War II art deriving highly charged, abstracted imagery from prehistoric, primitive, or folk sources of art. Rookmaaker took his students seriously as intellectual partners who could bring insight to him even as he sought to instruct them. He was not the kind of professor one dare not cross with a different opinion or perspective. He might not agree, but he would listen and question in a way that engendered growth and maturity in the thinking of his students. He could release his students to become who they were supposed to be. They did not have to be little clones of him.

Many students like Birtwistle became his friends. In this way much leads back again to J.P.A. Mekkes, Hans's wise mentor who knew how to grow reciprocity and collegiality out of differences in age and status and understanding. Mekkes mediated the mystery of mentoring to him well.

In the spirit of Mekkes, Hans also became the kind of person who saw promise in people before they completely recognized their own giftedness. Mekkes wrote when Hans received his doctorate that it pleased him to address him with a title he had always seen before his name. Rookmaaker often looked penetratingly into a person's potential in the same way that Mekkes gazed into his.

One of the most dramatic instances of Rookmaaker's talent scouting skill was with John Walford, who presently is professor of art history at Wheaton College in Illinois. In the late 1960s Walford was a young man living in London and trying to find himself and a purpose to live for. Although he had studied law for four years out of a sense of obligation to his family, his heart was not in it. He loved poking around art galleries and antique shops and began to dabble in buying and selling paintings, though there was no particular appreciation of art in his background.

In a conversation with a friend, Walford mentioned he had just bought a seventeenth-century Dutch painting. Immediately his friend suggested that he ought to meet Professor Rookmaaker and ask him about the picture. Little did he know what he was getting himself into. Rookmaaker not only responded to him— he turned up on his doorstep unexpectedly the morning after he and his friends had had an expansive evening in his flat. The dapper Dutch professor did not seemed bothered at all by the disarray of the young man's dwelling. As unpromising as an encounter like this might have seemed, it was the beginning of a course of care for Walford that would transform his life and give him a vocation.

By the time Rookmaaker met John Walford he was no stranger in Great Britain and knew dozens of young artists throughout the country. He frequently spoke at L'Abri Fellowship conferences at Ashburnham Place in Sussex. Meryl Fergus (later Doney), who served in the late 1960s as a traveling secretary for British art colleges with Inter-Varsity Fellowship (today UCCF) and her successor, Tony Wales, were nearly worn out from accompanying the Dutch dynamo around to speaking engagements at universities, colleges, and various conferences. After these events they would usually stay up nearly half the night with their guest speaker while he discussed ideas with students into the early morning hours over coffee or drinks in their lodgings or in some establishment that stayed open.

Rookmaaker drew close and was particularly encouraging to a number of young artists in the British Midlands. Today most of these artists have well-established reputations. Paul Martin, painter and printmaker as well as skilled in ceramics and sculpture, teaches at the Leith School of Art in Edinburgh and regularly receives commissions for his artwork, which has taken a direction informed by his adherence to the Orthodox Church. Martin Rose is a distinguished portrait painter with work hanging in the National Portrait Gallery in London. Kate Rose, printmaker, teaches art, as does her husband, Martin, at the Birkdale School (Sheffield) and has work in the collections of The Arts Council of Great Britain and the Sheffield Art Galleries.

Meryl Doney, who also benefited greatly from Rookmaaker's personal encouragement, has gone on to become an art impresario. With her husband, Malcolm, she co-hosts The Art Room (www.theartroom.net), a project to promote work by artists who revel in paint and to provide rich aesthetic nourishment for daily living rather than recondite ideas for cognoscenti. She has also coauthored with Malcolm *The Oxford Children's A to Z of Art* (1999). Meryl has written literally dozens of books on arts and crafts, serves on the research and development team of the Hayward Gallery on London's South Bank, and was involved in producing a major exhibition entitled "Presence: Images of Christ for the Third Millennium" (2004) at several English cathedral sites.

Superficiality was not in Rookmaaker's vocabulary. He exhibited incredible quality in his personal relationships, even as they expanded exponentially. He did not forget about the young fellow back in London who was not an artist but who loved art—namely, John Walford. From studying law, Walford had moved to teaching school. When Rookmaaker met up with him again, he bluntly told him he was wasting his time at teaching and that he should develop his God-given interests and come to study art history with him in the Netherlands. Walford was stunned at the thought. Could he not study art history in England, in his own mother tongue? Birtwistle seems to have been the one who challenged Walford by asking whether he would be willing to study theology with an atheist. His compa-

triot convinced him that being taught art history based on mate-
rialist suppositions was not much different. Finally Walford
braced himself to learn Dutch and submit himself to an invaluable apprenticeship of not only learning the academic requirements for a career in art history with his mentor, but a mission
to cultivate a love of the arts in the church that would lead to a
renewal of making art among Christians.

From Rookmaaker's well-planted seed of insight into
Walford's talent, a thriving and fruitful tree has grown. John is
the author of a major book on the great seventeenth-century
Dutch landscape artist Jacob van Ruisdael (*Jacob Van Ruisdael
and the Perception of Landscape*) (Yale, 1992) and also wrote
Great Themes in Art (Prentice-Hall, 2002), an important general
history of art, creatively structured thematically as well as
chronologically in order to engage students in reflecting through
art on spirituality, the self, nature, and the city. In turn, Walford
has poured out his Rookmaaker inheritance on his talented student James Romaine, who confidently careens along writing
crisp, culturally engaged art criticism even as he engages in serious art-historical research. Romaine's *Objects of Grace:
Conversations on Creativity and Faith* (Square Halo Books,
2002) brings together, without a whiff of self-consciousness, the
dynamic interaction of faith and art in the lives of ten very different types of artists. In an essay he wrote entitled, "Creator,
Creation, and Creativity" in *It was Good: Making Art to the
Glory of God*, edited by Ned Bustard (Square Halo Books,
2000), Romaine exegetes and illuminates the power of
Michelangelo's biblical vision to be vital down to our day and to
honor the Giver of all gifts even as multitudes of people mill
about the Sistine Chapel viewing his magnificent art.

The legacy of Hans Rookmaaker lives on in the freshness
and fidelity of work like this. Nor is it coincidental that Ned
Bustard, the publisher of Square Halo Books, has been deeply
influenced by Rookmaaker. Bustard says that after reading
Modern Art and the Death of a Culture, for a decade he kept that

tome on his nightstand, as it was one of the few credible books he could find linking being an artist and a Christian.

When Graham Birtwistle and then John Walford arrived in Holland to study with Rookmaaker, they encountered several worlds that their professor already inhabited and that they needed to discover. Hans did not have to go abroad to find an audience or following, though perhaps the prophet was not always appreciated as much as he could have been in his own land. He was a man in motion, incredibly involved in the life of his profession, country, causes, and church.

One of the first of his Dutch worlds that students like Birtwistle and Walford saw was Rookmaaker's university world at the Free University of Amsterdam. Hans was well-connected in the art-historical world both within Holland and abroad. His conversations rarely indicated these connections, but his letters and diaries show that he corresponded and/or met with many of the leading figures in art history of his day, such as Erwin Panofsky, Frederick Hartt, Jan Bialostocki, Linda Nochlin, and Herschel Chipp, to name but a few. He could have well found a position elsewhere than at the Free. He kept abreast of the ongoing research regarding the photographic documentation of the subject matter of art history at Leiden University, where he had formerly held a position, and communicated consistently with L.D. Couprie who was involved with this project. Today at the Free University there are still boxes and boxes of photos for this type of research that Rookmaaker collected. Further, he seems to have kept his hand in the International Association of Art Critics (AICA), founded in 1948/1949 to evaluate art criticism in relation to art history and to consider the responsibility of those who write on art in relation to artists and to the public. Administrative duties in his art history department, the university senate, and his own lectures, plus excursions with his students to local art institutions and abroad were more than enough to keep any mortal occupied.

To occupy him further, however, there were growing

unpleasant tensions within the department at the end of the 1960s and into the 1970s that everyone, students and staff, were aware of. While Rookmaaker had developed the department along with Bert van Swigchem and was drawing some of its best students, a significant sector of Dutch students was not happy. Many students were vocal in pointing out that they thought he spent too much time abroad, at L'Abri or with the "Rookies," his international students, even neglecting his scholarship. One can sense the confrontational spirit of the time in "Interview by Art History Students from the Free University." On these points he defended himself as needing to have awareness and contact with the wider world and to be hospitable to strangers and help them feel welcome. Still, even "Rookies" like Walford and Birtwistle wanted to see him devote himself more to scholarship.

Amidst these tensions he was not a paragon of perfection and probably was too reactive and not completely tactful. He had little sympathy for a trend he saw in many of the students at the Free University, moving away from appreciating the University's rich Reformed heritage and demanding a less specifically Christian education. He was in a painful bind. He had won his way to faith in the hardship of war and held dear every Christian principle on which the Free University was founded. Many of these students came from comfortable and typically Calvinist homes and were impelled in a diametrically different direction. They wanted out and not into Christianity (as they conceived it) and often associated it with authoritarianism and bourgeois morality. In Hans's mind they were trying to throw away the most important treasure in his life and did not understand how much he was a cobelligerent with them in regard to wanting to overthrow hypocrisy and exploitation.

Nevertheless, Rookmaaker had students in abundance, even if they were not all "official" students. Mature Dutch students such as Marc de Klijn and Hans van Seventer, who were formally enrolled (as we shall see), did get his message in a way that transformed their thinking and gave them clear direction for their lives. Ultimately there were no concrete walls around Hans's classroom or lecture hall. He soared in a less structured setting, a creative context that he played off as he taught. He seemed to be learning simultaneously as he was teaching, right where he was—driving along (he loved his Volvo and never let its service lapse), looking at a landscape, walking through a gallery, or partaking of a meal at Huize Kortenhoeve at Dutch L'Abri.

Bert van Swigchem, his colleague, put his finger exactly on Hans's leading teaching motif when he identified him as a bridge builder. More than anything Hans desired that there be a bridge between people on one side who recognized a Christian-oriented understanding of art history and theory and those on the other side who wanted to be Christian-oriented makers of art. Without this open spirit, Hans Rookmaaker simply would not have been Hans Rookmaaker! His legacy attests that many, many people found Rookmaaker not only to be a bridge builder for them, but indeed a veritable bridge himself.

For years, over and beyond his official academic activities, he traveled around the Netherlands speaking to all and sundry groups. His annual daybook agendas are filled with commitments showing how he crisscrossed the country from Groningen to 's-Gravenhage, from Amsterdam to Enschede to address gatherings and give lectures. Rookmaaker remained passionate about music and communicated memorably about it. From the titles of his talks noted in his dairy, there was quite a Dutch demand for topics like "Blues and Spirituals," "Jazz," "Black Music," and "Rock and Protest." In these years he also edited and annotated the Classic Jazz Masters reissued for the Riverside Series of Fontana Records.

Rookmaaker's calendars are also dotted with recurrent appointments to attend showings of films at various locations. For many years he contributed to national public life by serving on the Netherlands Film Censorship Board (Nederlandse Filmkeuring Kommissie/NFK). This by no means meant just a simple jaunt of an afternoon or evening to see a movie or two.

Rookmaaker wrestled intently with the issues of morality and censorship. His consciousness of the Calvinist heritage of the Netherlands made him immensely aware of the tradition of intellectual freedom and even an unusual toleration for pluralism going back to the seventeenth century in his native land. For example, he affirmed and was proud that René Descartes (1596–1650) had been able to live, work, and think freely for twenty years in Holland, whether he agreed or not with that philosopher's thought. Freedom must be delicately balanced with responsibility and the welfare of the public.

Rookmaaker did not have a ready-made Christian reaction to film, or for that matter to television and radio broadcasting. He scorned the attitude of Christians who righteously opted out altogether from seeing television or viewing films. It was better to have a voice in these matters, he said, even if collectively made judgments were not always completely correct. As a potent element of our culture, it was a part of our Christian calling, in his view, to give guidance in the area of the media and also for young people to have an exposure to them that was critically and constructively tempered so they could be inoculated, as it were, against their most pernicious effects.

Proactively he participated in creating programs on the radio, such as a series on African-American music, as well as supporting the general efforts of both Protestant networks (Nederlandse Christelijke Radio Vereniging in the mid-1960s and the Evangelische Omroep, which he helped to establish after its inception in 1970) in the Dutch pluralist broadcasting system. He also desired to see Christians make films that were life-affirming without avoiding difficult issues. (That part of his vision is probably only now beginning to take place.) Censorship was not just about sex but also about violence and sentimentality. It boggled his mind that North American viewers could be outraged at sex and nudity, yet tolerate before their eyes a steady stream of mayhem and obscenity consisting of horrific violence and saccharin sentimentality.

Although in the Netherlands today there is virtually no censorship of film—it being left up to distributors and broadcasters
on a voluntary basis to exercise discretion and judge suitability
for children—one must not be tempted to believe that
Rookmaaker's work in this area was totally in vain. He knew
public morality could not be legislated, but it could be shaped
and was being shaped rapidly, especially through new media.
The situation of reviewing films provided an important impetus
for him to articulate thoughts about the media and their technology that he may not have otherwise done. It is not an exag-
geration to say he pioneered in his own way every bit as much
as Marshall McLuhan, his famous contemporary, in opening up
understanding between the arts in popular culture and in so-
called high culture.

Although not unanimously appreciated by all of his students
at the Free University, Rookmaaker's commitment to contemporary cultural engagement in the light of biblical understanding did not go unnoticed by a number of thoughtful Dutch
students and artists coming to critical junctures in their careers
in the late 1960s and early 1970s. With the realities and issues
of this generation close to his heart, Hans began to stir the
Calvinist establishment to a fuller appreciation of art. He challenged them with the notion that art was as formidable a shaper
of culture as the political, economic, and scientific spheres that
they had integrated already into their lives. Those who only hear
the polemical voice of Rookmaaker, singing the glories of the
greatness of Calvinism's influence on the arts, especially the art
of seventeenth-century Holland, need also to hear the critical
voice of Rookmaaker calling the tradition to reform and to elaborate an understanding of the arts.

While it was untenable to believe that Calvin and the
Reformation had been entirely negative regarding the arts, he
clearly recognized that the history of the Reformed tradition had
a mixed record vis à vis the arts. With genuine anguish he spec-
ulated on how many people with artistic talents might have been

driven from the church, and even from Christ, by an oppressive cultural impoverishment due to a lack of clear affirmation of art in Calvinist churches. With conviction he worked to build structures and organizations to transform this situation by helping found the art history department at the Free University of Amsterdam (1964–1965), co-founding and being the first chairperson of the Christian Cultural Study Centre (Christelijk Cultureel Studiecentrum/CCS, 1964), leading eventually to the establishment of the Christian Academy for Visual Arts (Christelijke Academie voor Beeldende Kunsten/CABK, 1978) in Kampen, continuing the cultivation of the work of L'Abri Fellowship that he and his wife, Anky, had planted in the Netherlands in the late 1950s, and supporting initiatives in broadcasting and publishing in his homeland.

His call for change rang true. He was constructive and credible by his own commitment to labor in establishing structures to make a difference. Building on the outlook of people like Abraham Kuyper, Guillaume Groen van Prinsterer, and Willem Bilderdijk, Rookmaaker also crafted a vision of a particular kind of Dutch aesthetic sensibility. Deeply embedded in reality and in love for all of creation in every detail, he perceived a perspective disclosed by biblical contiguity that was neither ecclesiastical nor secular.

> Great freedom and openness to the entire creation, love for great and small, awareness of a certain hierarchy of values, avoidance of pomp and circumstance, sobriety that on the one hand avoids all idealization and on the other brooks no glorification of sin, emphasis on the human without heroizing while nevertheless acknowledging the importance of inward and outward struggle and taking an interest in the more intimate aspects of human relations—all this is ever the fruit for art of an approach to life nourished by the Scripture. (CW, 4:379)

Further along these lines, he endorsed the Kuyperian conviction that Calvinism helped open up art to the value of the seemingly unimportant and the beauty of everyday life and the humble landscape of his native land. In a reflection on the seventeenth-century Dutch landscape, he wrote:

> There was no longer any need to travel, to linger on mountains or wander in forests, to glorify the ruins of antiquity. And there was even less desire to violate that reality by romanticizing or poeticizing it (thereby turning it into something contrived). The 'ordinary' became relevant, meaningful, important. Out of a profound respect for this land (graciously given back to them by God, so that they could live in freedom), out of a deep reverence for this divine creation, out of a true love for reality in all its beauty and uniqueness, this art was born. (*CW*, 4:167)

Eventually Rookmaaker's extraordinary exposition of the ordinary could inspire artists who lived as far away as Oklahoma or Ontario to see significance in their own settings. But closer at hand, in Holland he was influencing a future generation on several fronts by being relevant to the present, critical of the past, and giving some hope for the future.

Marc de Klijn, Dutch artist and author, cherishes Rookmaaker's preserving effect on his life spiritually and intellectually. Marc was born in 1939 into a nonreligious, Jewish home. During the war his parents, with him as a small child in tow, managed to survive by being *onderduikers* who hid in homes at various addresses throughout the country. Many years later he began reviewing his parents' increased self-awareness of being Jewish after the war, as well as his personal losses, including the death of his mother just as he was completing his school examinations and going on to study graphic design in Basel, Switzerland.

On returning to the Netherlands in 1966, Marc took up the study of art history and philosophy in Amsterdam as he worked as a freelance designer. He also realized that he was in a mental crisis as to his personal identity and purpose for living. The turbulence of student unrest all around at the time contributed further to his explorations. Through contact with L'Abri Fellowship in Switzerland and with Rookmaaker at the Free University and L'Abri Fellowship in Holland, Marc found his way to belief and was baptized in 1971. He became a member (as Graham Birtwistle had) of the same denomination that Hans belonged to after 1968 (De Gereformeerde Kerk Vrijgemaakt Buiten Verband).

Over the course of the years, Marc de Klijn has been a dedicated custodian of Hans Rookmaaker's legacy. He has done this through the development of his own artistic work, writing, and teaching—supporting all endeavors to disseminate the thought and published works of Rookmaaker. His own achievements are considerable. He regularly exhibits his art and has his work reviewed. He is the author of many articles and several books on topics such as the influence of Calvinism on landscape painting, art and religion, and issues of faith. He has translated into Dutch an essay on topography by Eric Gill (1882–1940), an artist whose work Rookmaaker admired. He has written a book on the Shoah (2004), in which he engages in controversial contemporary interpretations of the horrendous suffering of the Jewish people during World War II.

De Klijn taught for some years at the Christian Academy for Visual Arts (Christelijke Academie voor Beeldende Kunsten/ CABK, 1978) in Kampen. He continues to maintain a studio in Kampen, but more recently he has supported an initiative of the Christian Artists Association for Visual Artists (Christian Artists Vereniging voor Beeldende Kunsten) with links to a broader arts organization, Christian Artists Association (Kunstenbond-CNV or CA for short), with headquarters in Rotterdam. Somewhat confusingly, the Christian Artists Association for Visual Artists is also called CABK. It represents an aspect of a wider attempt by CA to found a European Academy for Culture and the Arts based on a nontraditional educational model of mobile academic modules rather than a full-blown traditional system of formal programs anchored in one physical location. In the case of the visual arts, special seminars are arranged, some of which occur along with a host of other seminars in music, performance, media arts, and writing during a huge annual event sponsored by CA in various locations in the Netherlands.

In 2003 an intensive seven-day summer session in drawing and painting took place in the Carmelite Cloister at Drachten in the northern part of the country. As the older CABK follows a more institutionalized model of education for full-time students, the newer CABK seems set on being flexible and serving part-time students and working artists, as well as on restoring a healthy relationship between the church and art.

Britt Wikström, a Swedish-American sculptor living in Holland, is another artist influenced by Rookmaaker who has brought his work to bear on the CA. She has been key to bringing a strong sense and presence of the visual arts to CA. The CA, founded and assiduously developed since 1980 by Leen La Rivière, concert promoter and tour organizer with a knack for speaking and writing about creativity, music, and the arts, at first focused its annual seminar with subsidiary workshops on music followed by dance, mime, and theater. La Rivière affirmed the importance of the visual arts and encouraged Wikström to help pioneer this domain by drawing other outstanding artists for exhibitions and workshops. However, the reception of the visual arts in CA has not always been smooth. The stable place that they now seem to have in the organization probably can be traced back to a thread of credibility due to Rookmaaker's influence on the work and outlook of artists of the stature of Britt Wikström who are contributing to the maturing of this facet of the work of CA.

Rookmaaker's imprint is stamped all over Art Revisited, an enterprise created by Hans and JoAnn van Seventer to promote the work of artists who love reality and are devoted to a painterly depiction of common life and objects without slavish realism. Their media company, located in Aduard, near Groningen in the north of the Netherlands, published books, prints, and fine-art cards until 2002. They are also involved in making documentaries, mainly on themes related to the arts. Filmmaking is the fulfillment of a long-standing dream for Hans.

The van Seventers, both formal and informal former students of Hans and for some years senior workers at Dutch L'Abri, have been drawn close to a core of artists who met each other through Rookmaaker's work as a professor of art history at the Free University. A common chord was their appreciation of his exposition of the link between a work of art and an artist's beliefs and worldview. This group designated itself The Zwiggelte Group because they gathered often to discuss ideas and share their work at the van Seventers' and member artist Jan van Loon's farm in the small village of Zwiggelte near Westerbork.

In 1982 their work was presented together in an exhibition entitled "Reality Revisited," organized by the van Seventers and accompanied with a text written by JoAnn. "Reality Revisited" traveled in that year to the United States and introduced the work of Pit van Loo, Jan van Loon, Henk Helmantel, Rein Pol, Jan van der Scheer, and Jan Zwaan to a North American audience.

Today these artists (except Pit van Loo, who died in 1991) are all going strong in the Netherlands and have been joined by others inspired by a similar outlook. Their mutual affiliation with each other is quite loose now, except through their representation via reproduction by Art Revisited. All of them exhibit their original works regularly at galleries around the country, and some of them attract collectors from abroad.

Henk Helmantel's painting is rightly in high demand as it comes off his easel. His work genuinely invites comparison with the great Dutch masters in technique and sensibility, but only a superficial look at his work would suggest that he is only trying to emulate the art of a bygone age. He is *sui generis*. His composition, scale, and sparseness set him apart and show him to be a contemporary painter who is continually nourished by his artistic and spiritual heritage.

Van Loon's work expressively embraces the everyday world, from wine glasses to landscapes, dynamically ranging stylistically between naturalism and abstraction. For Rein Pol realism is more than a laborious substitute for a good photograph. His painting is quirky. One can find in it everything from elegant musical instruments to pig parts in formaldehyde. He also is a masterly portrait painter. Jan van der Scheer takes off in other directions. Inspired especially by Japanese art, van der Scheer paints exquisite watercolors with subjects ranging from oriental objects to plants and animals. Jan Zwaan is the son of a painter. When he was young, his father frequently took him with him as he painted in the open air. To this day he is dedicated to working outdoors. But it does mean painting quickly in the constantly changing moist climate of the Low Countries. His painting reflects his intoxication with light and texture.

Rookmaaker was ready to move on when he felt vision was lacking. Conversely, where he viewed vision was strong, he stayed the course (e.g., L'Abri Fellowship). When the Christian Cultural Study Centre (Christelijk Culturreel Studiecentrum/CCS) became less focused in terms of its Christian purpose (in his eyes), he became interested in helping develop and supporting the Christelijk Studiecentrum ICS (International Christian Study Centre), which began in 1970. Today this center carries on in a direction that Rookmaaker would no doubt be pleased with. As part of the Impact Network, it dynamically relates to multiple initiatives, including publications (*Impact* and *Cahier*), an informative and attractive web site (http://www.impactnetwerk.nl), lecture series, student groups, and annual conferences that seek to challenge and equip those aged twenty-five to forty to be faithful followers of Jesus Christ in their personal and professional lives, in communal life together, and in public.

It is also affiliated with the International Fellowship of Evangelical Student (IFES), the umbrella organization linking independent evangelical student movements around the world. Amidst ongoing study groups that it sponsors for lawyers, social workers, and other professionals, ICS hosted a special study group (2003/2004) on "The Complete Works of Hans R. Rookmaaker" and celebrated a Hans Rookmaaker day on November 1, 2003 (All Saints' Day).

Wim and Greta Rietkerk, much loved friends of the Rookmaakers and their gifted coworkers at Dutch L'Abri since 1974, steadfastly continue this work in the Netherlands, even as Wim over the years has also pastored a church and chaplained university students. Students and seekers still come to Huize Kortenhoeve, the big white, welcoming, eighteenth-century farmhouse at Eck en Wiel, set in the orchard heartland of Gelderland, to be quiet, to listen to recorded lectures, and to reflect creatively—in short, to retreat in order to go forward with renewed vigor. That the vitality of Dutch L'Abri continued after the death of Hans Rookmaaker is no better validated than in the publication of his *Complete Works*. In 1986/1987 Pieter and Elria Kwant spent a year there that seemed uneventful and unpromising, though in the course of it there increasingly arose a silent prayer in Pieter to do something with his life that would serve to build up others and honor God. He attests that this inchoate longing and supplication years ago gave him the desire to see Rookmaaker read widely again.

Though Pieter and Elria never knew Hans personally, they experienced him in the freshness of his writings. According to Elria, "He is always very 'present' in his writings—never just cold facts!" After considerable experience working with established publishers, Pieter and Elria launched their own press, Piquant, in 1999. The focused intent and scope of their commitment to serving those who serve the arts is unprecedented among Christian publishers.

In 1974 when the Rietkerks became full-time workers at Dutch L'Abri, Hans was happy to announce that they would be joined part-time by Henk Geertsema, a talented young assistant professor from the Free University who was willing to divide his time between teaching some courses at the university and being their coworker. Henk was someone who knew L'Abri Fellowship well, both in Switzerland and Holland. As a student of theology and philosophy he benefited from being able to sharpen his intellectual skills through the mentorship of both Rookmaaker and Schaeffer. Henk was a theologian (an expert in the theology of Jürgen Moltmann) and a specialist in Marxist philosophy, a combination that Hans saw as especially suited to the needs and concerns of young people at L'Abri at that time.

The promise Rookmaaker saw in Geertsema led to what some might consider a reckless career move on Henk's part, moving from a full-time university position to being a half-time Christian worker alongside teaching some courses in philosophy. But this move has today been vindicated. Geertsema is recognized as a distinguished philosopher whose writings range over such topics as modern culture, the human character of knowing, humanity in scholarship, faith and life, and the meaning of freedom for the study of the social sciences. Dr. H.G. Geertsema now occupies the Dooyeweerd Chair of Philosophy at the Free University of Amsterdam, as well as serving as *bijzondere hoogleraar* in Reformational Philosophy at the universities of Groningen and Utrecht.

Rookmaaker's academic mentoring was not lavished only on men. Dr. Mary Leigh Morbey is associate professor of culture and technology at York University in Toronto. She possesses an eye-popping resumé of awards and publications. Her writings span such subjects as cybercolonialism, electronic technologies and the visual arts, and gender and are on the forefront of scholarship on technology and culture.

Mary Leigh does not hesitate for a second to acknowledge that Hans Rookmaaker was a major shaper of her life in her early twenties when she studied with him in the faculty of art history at the Free University (1973–1976), receiving her Doctor's degree there in 1976. She says:

As my professor, he literally taught me how to 'think' in deeper and more nuanced ways, and did this in a most gentle and supportive manner. He did not differentiate between male and female graduate students at that time in the early 1970s as many in the academy did. This was most helpful to my development and I imagine the development of other female students with whom he worked.

As a Christian scholar, he continually pressed the meaning and purpose of life given to Christian believers and this has subsequently shaped all aspects of my life: my marriage, family, academic/scholarly work at every institution I have served whether it be Redeemer University College or York University.

She also appreciates that Rookmaaker introduced her to Calvin Seerveld, who mentored her further, especially in regard to carefully crafting her scholarship. In sum, they both have left their legacy in teaching her how, in turn, to mentor her students Christianly.

One must not forget the academic achievements of Rookmaaker's children either. A visit to The National Library of the Netherlands in The Hague will find publications of all three of his children there. Both of Hans's sons—Hans, Junior and Kees—have doctorates from the University of Utrecht. Hans, Junior dedicated his book *Towards A Romantic Conception of Nature: Coleridge's Poetry Up to 1803* (1984) to the memory of his father, "whose ideas and love of learning have always been a source of inspiration to me." Inspired by stories his father shared of the serious naturalist and environmental pursuits of his colonial administrator grandfather, whom he never knew, Kees has gone on to be a world authority on the history of zoos and on the rhinoceros in captivity and has written several books. Kees has also written on his grandfather's expedition to Rintja in the Dutch Indies in 1927 to capture twelve of the largest of the earth's monitor-type lizards, known as Komodo dragons. Marleen has made her mark in pioneering serious reflection from a Christian perspective on popular music. She has also taken on the mammoth task of gathering all her father's works together, seeing to their translation into English, and editing them. All of this is a testament to their father's inspiration as well as to their filial respect for him.

Most of the Americans and Canadians who were influenced by Rookmaaker were introduced to him in the 1970s when he increasingly gained a public presence and profile in North America. He had written articles for *Christianity Today*, published his best-selling book *Modern Art and the Death of a Culture* (InterVarsity Press, 1970; Crossway Books, 1994), and was highly visible as a close associate of Francis Schaeffer. From 1970 to 1977, the year of his death, he traveled each year except 1971 to North America. During these years he forged many friendships with individuals as well as links with Christian institutions in both the United States and Canada.

A few North Americans who were in Reformed circles or who were living or traveling in Europe learned of him in the 1960s. Calvin Seerveld was an exception. He had met Rookmaaker in the late 1950s when he was living in Holland. T. Grady Spires, professor of philosophy (emeritus) at Gordon College (Wenham, Massachusetts), was in touch with Rookmaaker from the time of his first visit to the USA in 1961. In the mid-1960s he collaborated on translating "Let's Sing the Old Dr Watts: A Chapter in the History of Negro Spirituals," which appeared in *The Gordon Review* (1966). Grady also tried to recruit Rookmaaker to teach at Gordon, but there was not enough institutional will at that time at Gordon to do this. Grady's abiding friendship with Hans strengthened his tenacity to make the arts more visible at Gordon and eventually put them on the college's agenda in a serious way. Gordon College now has an impressive faculty of art and a well-equipped arts center in its own building. It also gives an institutional home to Christians in the Visual Arts (CIVA), the premier place in North America for Christian artists, art teachers, critics, collectors, and other lovers of the visual arts to come together from across the whole denominational spectrum to be encouraged to excellence in their work and faithfulness to Christ in their daily walk. Although CIVA was not founded out of a direct impulse related to Rookmaaker, many of its earliest leaders as well as some of its present leadership found their formation significantly shaped by him and/or his thinking.

Ted Prescott has chaired and teaches in the Art and Theatre Departments at Messiah College in Grantham, Pennsylvania. He is a sculptor and art critic with many prestigious commissions and literary credits to his name. Ted has also been a president of CIVA. The affirmation that Rookmaaker gave to him and his wife, Catherine, a gifted portrait and landscape painter, was incisive.

In the autumn of 1970 the Prescotts went for six months to L'Abri in Switzerland. They were filled with enthusiasm for their newly found faith and were deeply affected by the countercultural revolution of the 1960s. Ted was a newly minted MFA in sculpture and trying to figure out what he was supposed to do. Both Prescotts had many doubts and insecurities concerning what they were doing and where they were going. Then Francis Schaeffer arranged for them to spend time with Rookmaaker. When it was time for Hans to return home, they drove him to the airport in Geneva. In a characteristic gesture that he would make on many occasions with many people, he suggested to them that they could stop at the municipal museum of Geneva on the way. His humor and vitality affected them. His ideas were totally new and removed from what they had received as students. They were challenged. Equally as characteristic of Rookmaaker, he encouraged them to find their own way and not accept everything he said as being from on high.

As their time to return to the USA approached, they longed to linger in Europe. Hans invited them to stay in Holland and even found inexpensive accommodations for them. Ted was stunned when Rookmaaker arranged for him to have an interview with the Ministry of Culture in the Netherlands regarding studying art restoration. Even more amazingly, after the interview the ministry was willing to have the Dutch government send him to Italy for two years to gain competencies, if he could wait six months for a new fiscal year. However, their coffers were completely depleted, and they had to head home. But before their departure, Hans arranged for them to spend an evening in a charming thatched-roof house near the Amstel River with some of his students. On that memorable occasion, they met someone who subsequently became their deep and lifelong friend— namely, John Walford. Although they may have wondered what their life would have been like had they spent two years in Italy, little did either they or Walford know then that John would come to spend his entire teaching career in America.

As theology was not Rookmaaker's forte, we can now see from this point in time something that probably would have surprised him greatly: his enrichment of theological education through people bringing fresh perspectives to this field through the arts. The list is sizable.

Bill Edgar, a musician and a professor of theology at Westminster Theological Seminary (Philadelphia), was immensely appreciative as a musically gifted young man, beginning his undergraduate studies at Harvard, to find someone like Rookmaaker, who was interested in genuine jazz the same way he was and who generously gave him old jazz recordings in 1962. Subsequently Edgar has written books in both English and French relating music to Christian understanding.

In 1967 Thena Ayres, assistant professor of adult education and dean of students at Regent College and at that time a recent university graduate, met Rookmaaker at L'Abri in Switzerland and soon cemented a friendship with him by meeting him accidentally again shortly afterward in Rome in an art gallery while he was on excursion there with his art history students. Spontaneously Rooky invited her to come along with the group. Italian art and opera, guided by a Continental professor and his energetic students, was a heady and inspiring mix for a young woman from western Canada. Thena was struck immediately by the fact that he related his scholarly learning to his Christian understanding. Furthermore, she saw that his perspective on the visual arts engaged the dilemma of being modern—alone and alienated from God. She also noted how he encouraged artists and went out of his way for his students, qualities of mentoring that she, like Mary Leigh Morbey, has absorbed into her own practice of teaching.

In 1967 William Dyrness was a theological student in his last year at Fuller Theological Seminary in Pasadena, California, and had heard of the Dutch art-historian through Francis Schaeffer. In that year Bill wrote a letter to Rookmaaker to explore the idea of his coming to study with him, explaining that he did not want to leave the field of theology but wanted to see if theology could enrich his understanding of aesthetics. After an interlude of study in Amsterdam with decisive direction from Rookmaaker, Dyrness eventually went on to complete a doctorate on the art and theology of Georges Rouault at the University of Strasbourg in France. Also of great benefit to him as he was setting out were other young scholars such as John Walford, Maria Dellù (today Dr. Maria Walford-Dellù), and Graham Birtwistle, to whom Hans introduced him. As a professor of theology and an academic administrator whose career has taken him from Asia Theological Seminary in the Philippines, New College Berkeley (Berkeley, California), and full circle back to Fuller, Bill Dyrness continues to make a monumental contribution to theology and the arts. In the 1960s the arts were nowhere on the theological horizon of Fuller Seminary. Today they are highly visible, with a center devoted to them and an annual arts and film festival to boot.

Rookmaaker's influence on the direction of the arts at Regent College was formative as well. The whole conception of Regent College was innovative. In 1969, when it was founded, there was not another postgraduate theological institution that was aimed specifically at equipping laypeople rather than ministers or theologians with a theological education. Although the arts were not a conscious part of the agenda of the new endeavor, there was great openness from the founding faculty, particularly James Houston and Ward Gasque, to the arts as a vital impulse within the community.

Prior to coming to Vancouver to help establish the college, Ward and Laurel Gasque were living in England. At that time they had opportunity to host Francis and Edith Schaeffer in their home in Manchester and also to attend a spring conference of L'Abri Fellowship at Ashburnham Place in Sussex in March 1968. There they were introduced to Hans Rookmaaker and were immediately impressed by his academic sophistication and utterly refreshing approach to thinking about art and culture and Christian belief in contemporary society. Following the conference they were delighted to join him on one of his inimitable walking art history courses at the Tate Gallery in London. After that the Gasques could hardly wait to sign him up to teach at a Regent College Summer School.

So it was that Rookmaaker became a featured part of the Regent College Summer Schools (1970, 1972, 1974). Further incentive for him to come to Vancouver was his friendship with Thena Ayres, who by that time had returned from Europe and her graduate studies at Covenant Theological Seminary in St. Louis and was on the staff of Inter-Varsity Christian Fellowship in Canada. Thena was a great supporter of the fledgling college and was excited that the arts would be encouraged so substantially by having someone of Hans's stature leading the way. Other friends living in British Columbia were the poet Hannah van der Kamp and artist Robert Main. When Hannah and Robert married, they made sure it was in the summertime when Rooky was around. Enthusiasm abounded, and in 1970 on Hans's first stint at Regent, he brought Anky, Hans, Kees, and Marleen with him to Vancouver for a summer vacation that went down in the family annals as truly memorable.

Rookmaaker's summer sessions at Regent were legendary. The peppery little professor with the pipe might say almost anything to provoke a good discussion. Jaws sometimes dropped at images he showed in his slide presentations. He could be tough on his projectionists too. One of the survivors of this experience was Dal Schindell, then a student at Regent College who was also an artist. After Rooky, there was no turning back for Dal. As soon as he could scrape up the funds, he was off to England to continue his studies at Sheffield Polytechnic, where he soon became a member of the H.R. Rookmaaker-inspired artists' group there that hearkened back to the days when Hans was shepherded around the British Midlands by Meryl Doney and Tony Wales. Other unsuspecting Regent Summer School students to come under the influence of Rookmaaker have been Roger Feldman, Wayne Roosa, Mary Ellen Ashcroft, and Betty Spackman. In 1970 New York artist Chris Anderson flamboyantly flew into Vancouver simply to meet Rookmaaker.

As a result of meeting Rookmaaker, Feldman ceased studying theology and devoted himself to becoming a sculptor. Presently he is professor of art at Seattle Pacific University. Wayne Roosa is an art historian teaching at Bethel University (St. Paul, Minnesota) and author of numerous publications. His forthcoming book is entitled *The Quiet Heresy: Biblical Themes in Contemporary Art*. Mary Ellen Ashcroft also teaches at Bethel University. She is a professor of English literature and a prolific author herself. Spackman is an artist who has gone on to exhibit her work in Canada, the Netherlands, and Austria and to teach for many years at Redeemer University College (Ancaster, Ontario) and now at Trinity Western University (Langley, British Columbia).

Anderson has received many grants and awards for her work, which has appeared in over fifty public and corporate collections. She has exhibited her painting work in the USA and abroad and taught at many institutions, including Regent College. Schindell has ended up back at Regent College, where he serves as Director of Publications, Director of the Lookout Art Gallery, and Instructor in Christianity and Art in a program at the college that is burgeoning. Formerly Regent College Summer

School students under Rookmaaker, Roosa and Ashcroft have returned to Regent a number of times to teach a new generation of summer school students there.

Whether teaching at a summer session, giving special lectures, or going to a conference sponsored by L'Abri, Rookmaaker always managed to squeeze an enormous amount of travel in between his destinations when he was in North America. Philadelphia artist Bettina Clowney remembers spending a whole day with Rookmaaker at the National Gallery of Art in Washington, DC, as well as a visit to the Philadelphia Museum of Fine Arts. Although her work has taken off in some directions that she feels Rookmaaker would have considered "mystical" (she has studied icon writing with the Russian iconographer Vladislav Andrejev for a decade), she says he was very influential in her life and art. When she met him, she was a new Christian and a very dedicated painter and student of art history. His dry humor delighted her. She comments, "His enthusiasm and deep humanity and humility impressed me. He heard my aspirations with emotional generosity [and gave me] huge permission [to seek] truth, life, and God in my work . . . to be myself with my work and with God."

Art historian Lee Hendrix, Curator of Drawings at the J. Paul Getty Museum, met Rookmaaker through L'Abri connections in Tennessee as she was completing her undergraduate years at Vanderbilt University. After foundational graduate studies with Rookmaaker at the Free University, she was well prepared to do a doctorate at Princeton University on the Flemish late Renaissance painter Joris Hoefnagel and to continue on to an outstanding scholarly career. In Calgary, Alberta, in 1975 Dutch-born Canadian artist Gerard Pas caught up with Rookmaaker after hitchhiking his way across half of Canada to meet him. By Pas's own admission, he pushed the provocative and even distasteful in his art so that even after considerable spiritual transformation he still shocked many people by some of his habits of language and life. But as Bettina Clowney discovered, he too found that Rookmaaker looked and listened at a deeper level to his aspirations.

Rookmaaker was not shocked and seriously engaged Pas in an intellectually nuanced way so that he could be free as a Christian to pursue complex issues in his art without superficiality or simplistic solutions.

In the early 1970s in the midst of the free speech movement at the University of California at Berkeley, Sharon Gallagher, film critic and editor of *Radix* magazine, felt tremendously heartened when Rookmaaker came to Berkeley to "support the troops" there who were seeking a third way between the radical right and the radical left—a way that showed committed Christians were also radical in the sense of going to the roots of their faith in seeking social justice and embracing the arts for the benefit of all. Hans gave informal talks and a lecture on the UCB campus. Sharon interviewed him for publication. Berkeley performance artists Susan and David Fetcho found Rookmaaker's honesty and humanity reassuring in its spontaneous expression. Being in Berkeley gave Hans a strong dose of what the dynamics of protest were like at America's most influential public university.

But Rookmaaker was to have an impact and develop interests even farther afield than Berkeley. In 1970 Kefa Sempangi, a Ugandan artist whom Hans had invited to study with him, arrived at the Free University. Hans had met Kefa on one of his visits to the UK. The young Ugandan had been doing postgraduate studies at the Royal College of Art in London. Hans and Anky welcomed Kefa and his wife, Penina, with warmth and hospitality. They were eager to learn more about Africa from the Sempangis. Hans soon asked questions about art and culture in Africa to gain a better understanding than he would have had solely by reading scholarly texts. Kefa was a firsthand informant. Understanding art in contemporary non-Western cultures was a significant area of inquiry that Hans was developing before he died. This subject also interested Bill Dyrness, who had come with broad missional interests in art and culture to study with Hans earlier.

When Kefa and Penina returned to Uganda in 1971, Hans and Anky did not forget them. They supported Kefa in his academic work in the Fine Art Department of Makerere University (Kampala) as well as in the benevolent work he took up for street children during the time of severe oppression under the terrorist regime of Idi Amin. And in 1974 they enabled the Sempangis to leave their country and find refuge abroad until they were able to return in 1979. During the depths of the brutality of Amin's tyranny in Uganda, Hans was unable to visit his student's homeland, but he did visit Kenya. In 1976 he accompanied Anky on a trip she made there in connection with her Redt een Kind work. This opportunity gave him a brief but rich experience of Africa. Traveling with Anky gave him an advantage to see African life and culture more from the perspective of a participant than he would have had as a conventional visitor. Coming less than a year before his death, his first direct encounter with African culture in context was only beginning to fertilize his reflection on art and faith in the non-Western world.

In Hans's time at Swiss L'Abri, he may not have been aware of another African student who listened attentively and deeply to all that he had to say. Kwame Bediako, a Ghanian, destined to become one of Africa's foremost theologians, sat rapt for a week at Hans's feet in Huémoz. Bediako went on to earn doctorates in French literature from the University of Bordeaux and in theology from the University of Aberdeen. Today he is noted for penetratingly exploring the experience of African identity as it embraces the Christian faith. He serves as the Director of the Akrofi-Christaller Memorial Centre for Mission Research and Applied Theology in Akropong-Akuapem, Ghana, and is a minister of the Presbyterian Church of Ghana with a worldwide reputation as an interpreter of African culture and Christianity. Bediako honors Rookmaaker's work and acknowledges its influence on him at a seminal stage in his development. He feels he is doing for Africa what he believes Rookmaaker was attempting to do for Western culture. Following in the footsteps of Abraham Kuyper and other distinguished Reformed thinkers, Bediako gave the Stone Lectures at Princeton Theological Seminary in the autumn of 2003.

Rookmaaker's impact in Great Britain has been touched on already, but it deserves to be looked at again as it continues to grow. Peter Heslam writes, "It is Hans Rookmaaker . . . who was largely responsible for establishing the Kuyperian tradition in Britain . . . and inspiring a whole generation of Christian art students with his vision of thinking about the arts, and indeed practicing the arts, from a committed Christian perspective." While broadly speaking what Heslam says is true, there was also prepared ground for Hans when he planted his seed of Neo-Calvinism in British evangelical circles primarily associated with Inter-Varsity Fellowship (today UCCF). Several factors contributed to these favorable conditions.

First of all, when Rookmaaker arrived on the scene in Britain in the late 1960s, biblical and theological scholarship by evangelical Christians was gaining credibility. Foremost among these scholars was F.F. Bruce, the John Rylands Professor of Biblical Criticism at the University of Manchester. He had been one of the founders of both the Theological Students Fellowship and the Tyndale Fellowship for Biblical Research, groups that gave a sense of confidence to a new generation of evangelical scholars, and was one of the authors of the earliest influential scholarly and nontechnical books that were being published by Inter-Varsity Press. Although he was neither a Presbyterian nor a Calvinist in the strict sense, Bruce had recently taken over the editorship of *The Evangelical Quarterly*, described as a "Journal for the Defence of the Reformed Faith."

When Bruce and Rookmaaker came to know each other at Regent College in 1970, there was instant mutual respect and warmth between them. At the same time, there was a renewal of Calvinist theology in the UK, pioneered by the study groups initiated by Martin Lloyd-Jones and later dominated by J.I. Packer, and the reissuing of older Calvinist works by Banner of Truth. Secondly, coupled with this changing intellectual climate among evangelicals was an eager audience poised for just the resources Rookmaaker could bring to them. The evangelical literature coming off the press focused primarily on biblical and theological studies rather than on issues of contemporary life and culture. Thus there were leaders of the younger generation, people such as Meryl Doney, Tony Wales, and David and Pat Alexander, who were ready to leap from the margins of cultural discourse to direct engagement. Rookmaaker brought the right blend of intellectual substance, along with missional dynamism, that they were looking for but could hardly have believed existed before they saw Rookmaaker in action. They also loved the fact that he blew away with the smoke from his pipe the sentimental, pietistic cant and niceties that evangelicals were prone to and cut to the real issues at stake in the culture. Each of the individuals mentioned above went on to careers in writing and publishing that greatly broadened the scope of Christian publishing in the UK.

Thirdly, and perhaps most importantly and decisively for Rookmaaker's introduction to the UK, was a group of friends with a Reformational outlook in Britain who connected directly with Dooyeweerdians in the Netherlands. Key among this group was David Hanson, today a physician specializing in ear, nose, and throat and a keen Christian layman living in Leeds. David says he knew about Rookmaaker before he met him through his connection with the highly prized Riverside Classical Jazz recordings as well as by the reputation of his other writings, the contents of which were conveyed to him by his friends who read Dutch.

Rookmaaker seems to have invited himself to Britain. In 1966 Hans wrote to David Hanson that he would like to come and stay with him and "would you please find some art students, artists, art teachers [for me] to talk to?" David is still not sure who had given Hans his name—possibly J.D. Dengerink or Henk van Riessen, Dutch philosophers whom he knew. As Hanson sprang into networking to make arrangements for Hans's visit, little did he realize what an important gateway he was providing for Rookmaaker's influence in Great Britain. Of long-term significance was the contact he made that paved the way for Hans to visit the Birmingham Art College, where he met Peter Smith, Kate and Martin Rose, and Paul and Sandra Martin, who at that time were students there. As noted above, members of this group have become well-established artists. Without in the least being slavish, their work is still attuned to the philosophical and artistic implications of what Rookmaaker was saying and continues to say through his works.

Rookmaaker's direct influence on Hanson was strong. Hanson calls it "a powerful factor in moving me further and further away from dualist pietism." Hans persuaded Hanson that "the missionary position" was of small consequence unless it was linked with commitment to be a transforming presence in civic society, professional life, and one's own neighborhood. In turn, the Reformational and Kuyperian perspective conveyed by Hans has helped inspire David and his wife, Ruth, who holds a postgraduate degree in psychology, to develop this perspective within the West Yorkshire School of Christian Studies (WYSOCS).

The multiple trips Hans made to England each year in the last decade of his life called for a lot of juggling and the utmost economical use of his time when he was in the UK. In the late 1960s a small interest in the arts was beginning to blossom among evangelical Christians. The actor Nigel Goodwin was filled with passion to see performers, artists, and musicians with strong faith in the practice of their professional lives. In November 1967 he met Rookmaaker on a visit to L'Abri in Switzerland. His relationship with Hans never faltered as he learned from him, and his friendship with him became deeper with every passing year.

Prior to 1967 only a few art students in Birmingham associated with the Reformed tradition seemed to know about Rookmaaker. While Rookmaaker's name was closely associated with Francis Schaeffer, he did not come to Britain riding on his coattails. L'Abri Fellowship was not even formally established in Britain at the times of Hans's early visits. It did, however, have a small study base in a house church in Ealing in the western part of London. Nigel nurtured friendships there with Sylvester and Janet Jacobs and Linette and Joe Martin, whom he had met in Switzerland. They had strong interests in the arts. Sylvester was an American photographer. Linette was a dancer and writer. Later she wrote the first biography of Rookmaaker (*Hans Rookmaaker: A Biography*, Hodder & Stoughton /InterVarsity Press, 1979), but even before that, Sylvester's story of encountering hostility and rejection as a black person growing up in the United States (*Born Black*, Hodder & Stoughton, 1977). Colin Duriez, author and literary entrepreneur, had also been with them at Swiss L'Abri in 1967.

Momentum was mounting. After accompanying Rookmaaker to Birmingham, Meryl Doney was introducing him to ever-widening circles of students. In 1968 Inter-Varsity Fellowship (UCCF) sponsored a major conference on vocation in Keele. Rooky was the featured speaker and proved to be the galvanizing element. He provoked thinking and was a catalyst to action. Increasingly, art students were gathering, and Rookmaaker was speaking at conferences in different parts of the country. From 1968 onward, larger events and longer-term ventures were embarked on.

Meanwhile, Nigel Goodwin's vision matched the concern of a group of Christians that included world-famous rock singer Cliff Richard, who had recently come to faith, in desiring to see a meeting-place where those active in the arts could talk and laugh, weep and work, and pray. In 1971 Nigel joined forces with these friends in establishing the Arts Centre Group (ACG). Nigel, newly married, worked with his wife, Gillie, in directing the operations and hosting events at the ACG's first location in

Kensington. Later the ACG moved to premises in Waterloo, with The Old Vic and The Young Vic theatres close by, and Nigel and Gillie were gradually released after painstaking pioneer labor to a broader ministry that enabled them eventually to travel more and encourage countless artists around the world. ACG saw a host of extremely talented people being influenced by Rookmaaker at the threshold of their careers in the arts come through its doors. Some of them were: Norman Stone (filmmaker), Murray Watts (director and writer for theater and film), and Malcolm Doney (artist and author).

The ACG continues to provide support to Christian artists and includes a mentoring program and a quarterly magazine called *ArtsMedia*. The editor, David Porter, and his wife, Tricia, who is a professional photographer, were both encouraged to make the arts their life's work through their early and formative contact with Rookmaaker. As an expression of their esteem for Hans, their book *Over the Bent World*, an introduction to the life and work of Gerard Manley Hopkins, was dedicated to Rookmaaker.

Other organizations to arise that were influenced by Rookmaaker were the Institute for Contemporary Christianity in London and *Third Way* magazine. Thirty years ago the Greenbelt Arts Festival started primarily as a Christian music festival with about fifteen hundred young people stomping in soggy Suffolk fields. In the 1980s up to thirty thousand would come. Located today at the Cheltenham Racecourse, thousands still show up (many of them the mature youth of yesteryear with their children) for a celebration of the arts through exhibits, workshops and seminars, concerts, and corporate worship. This event shows the lifting of the stigma and suspicion of the arts among conservative Christians as well as a broadened understanding and appreciation of cultural engagement in the UK these days. The founding father of the festival, John Peck, a poet and pastor, relished the work of Hans Rookmaaker and Francis

Schaeffer. Peck also lends his wisdom to Christian Artists (CA) in the Netherlands.

Two other initiatives that bear an influence of Rookmaaker in the UK are the Leith School of Art (LSA) in Edinburgh and the Theology Through the Arts (TTA) project, now a part of the Institute for Theology, Imagination and the Arts (ITIA), a new research unit based at the University of St Andrews with links at the University of Cambridge. Philip Archer, artist and principal of LSA, attests that Rookmaaker set them on a path that they continue to travel. Eleven years ago, after the tragic deaths of Mark and Lottie Cheverton, founders of the school, Philip was invited to head its administration. While Archer knew Rookmaaker, he is glad to have Paul Martin teaching alongside him who knew him better. Paul believes "Rookmaaker was one of the most important influences of the 1960s and 1970s beginning the work of 'justifying the ways of God to man' through the arts."

Jeremy Begbie, theologian and musician, the creative shaper of Theology Through the Arts, is not only one of a sizable list of theological educators influenced by the thought of Hans Rookmaaker—he is himself a sizable industry in theology and the arts! Begbie spearheads research colloquia, publishing projects, and experiments in artistic creation, as well as the supervision of graduate research students in theology and the arts. He also does a great deal of public lecturing and scholarly writing. Today the TTA project he launched at the University of Cambridge is more like a movement—a movement to think differently about the arts in relation to theology. It addresses the abstraction of a theology of the arts that tends to wander off into woolly vagueness on its head and brings into focus a genuine respect for concrete works of art and artistic practices that can be theologically explored and exegeted with precision for their intellectual meaning, cultural relevance, and spiritual discovery.

In this lies one of the most important affinities TTA has with Rookmaaker's thought. One might almost say that it took a Jeremy Begbie to come along to give a name to the approach to the arts of which Rookmaaker was a master practitioner. Neither the breadth of Rookmaaker's intellectual interests and cultural concerns, nor his deep regard for philosophical issues ever took him away from the concrete and the specific, from cultural analysis or philosophizing through the consideration of particular works of art embedded in history or present reality. He never took works of art as a pretext for explaining or illustrating his ideas or theories. Begbie's discussion of Rookmaaker and art in his book *Voicing Creation's Praise* (T & T Clark, 1991) is a key document in placing Hans's work in the context and tradition of Dutch Neo-Calvinism.

Besides Begbie, many other musicians have felt the influence of Rookmaaker. Ric Ashley, professor of music and composition at Northwestern University (Evanston, Illinois), has spent extended time in the Netherlands and studied Hans's works in Dutch. In respect for his time at Dutch L'Abri and the benefit of Rookmaaker's conversations with him, Peter Anthony Monk, a contemporary composer, dedicated one of his works to him. More popularly oriented musicians have also appreciated him. In 1985 Garth Hewitt, sometimes described as a British activist-troubadour counterpart to Bruce Cockburn, dedicated his album *Alien Brain* to Hans. The late Mark Heard, perhaps one of Christian rock's most respected singers and writers, clearly expressed his appreciation for Rookmaaker. Hans's impact has long reverberated for British poets and writers including Steve Turner and the American-based Steve Scott as well.

How does one sum up the influence of Hans Rookmaaker's life? Several impressions of the man and his work stand out. First and strikingly, there was his refreshing modesty, lack of pretension, and willingness to be a servant of the arts and artists, and in this, a servant of Christ and his church. This set him apart from many of his academic peers who were sequestered in their professional work. Secondly, there was his love of life—all of life: music, art, good food and drink, good conversation, new experiences, new friends. Thirdly, he had the ability to discern the gifts that young men and women whom he met along the way possessed and to encourage them to move in the direction that would best develop their God-given gifts, giving them freedom to be themselves. Fourthly, he was a willing mentor to many young adults, both scholars and artists, in a wide variety of vocations. It is especially noteworthy that he mentored a remarkable number of women as well as men. This was unusual for his time, as it is perhaps even today. Fifthly, he was a bridge builder, linking the scholarship of art to the work of artists, celebrating all of the arts and developing a broad mastery of different eras and disciplines, communicating effectively with both scholars and the general public. Sixthly, he sought to reclaim the arts for the Reformed Christian faith. Although there is still much land to be possessed, the contributions of Rookmaaker's intellectual and spiritual children and grandchildren bear witness to the progress that has been made in the past half century and give much hope for the next. Seventhly, he was committed to living and thinking as a Christian in the midst of the world rather than in a cloistered sectarian shelter. And he challenged all who came under his influence to do likewise.

In the first three months of 1977, Hans had been busy as usual. The first of January was a special day, not just because it was the first day of the year, but also because the Chapel in the Barn at Eck en Wiel was dedicated, and Edith and Fran Schaeffer were there from Switzerland to help celebrate the occasion. It was the last time they were to see Hans. Just a few days later Hans was off to the USA. For many years he had attended a gathering of the Association for Reformational Philosophy at that time of year. But he did not do this in 1977. Eleanor DeLorme, a friend who is an art historian at Wellesley College in Massachusetts, remembers that she and her husband drove him to the airport for his flight back to Holland. Soon he was going full tilt back into university life, and yet at a bit of a remove from it, as he and Anky had been living in Ommeren, not far from L'Abri at Eck en Wiel since 1975, and it was necessary for Hans to commute. Happily, however, he enjoyed staying overnight when he did go into Amsterdam with Graham Birtwistle, who had taken over the Walfords' charming cottage near the Amstel River. He had plans to go to Edinburgh in May and then to Canada in July to teach in Ontario and possibly go on to Vancouver.

On Sunday morning, March 13 the Rookmaakers went to church in the newly dedicated chapel at L'Abri. Wim Rietkerk preached. The air was crisp, and the day was quiet. They went home for a peaceful afternoon. But Hans did not feel well. By 8 P.M. in the evening he was gone, dying with an expression of surprise and delight, without any sense of horror.

From the time of his conversion Hans was practicing prophetic preparedness: "Watch therefore—for you do not know when the master of the house will come, in the evening, or at midnight, or at cockcrow, or in the morning." How like his beloved Bach cantata, *Wachet auf, ruft uns die Stimme*. Or, *Gottes Zeit is die allerbeste Zeit*.

On Wednesday, March 16, Hans's funeral took place in the pre-Reformation church in Eck en Wiel. Wim preached on, "'Blessed indeed,' says the Spirit, 'that they may rest from their labors, for their deeds follow them'" (Revelation 14:13b)—the text chosen by his family and cited at the beginning of this chapter. Hans's request for his funeral was honored with Mahalia Jackson's rendition of

> *Soon one evening, I'm going home to live on high. . . .*
> *I'm gonna move on up a little higher. . . .*
> *It will be always howdy, howdy and never goodbye.*

Hans was buried in the small cemetery in Eck en Wiel. His gravestone is simple and completely open in the middle—a fitting memorial for an open life.

APPENDIX I:
CHRONOLOGY

1848 Henderik Roelof Rookmaaker (1848–1905), grandfather of H.R.R., born. Later became an Assistant-Resident in the colonial administration of the Dutch East Indies.

1887 August 21. Henderik Roelof Rookmaaker, Senior, father of H.R.R., born. Later became Resident in the colonial administration of the Dutch East Indies.

1890 March 17. Theodora Catharina Heitink, H.R.R.'s mother, born.

1897 J.P.A. (Johan Pieter Albertus) Mekkes, mentor and friend of H.R.R., born.

1911 H.R. Rookmaaker, Senior graduates from the University of Leiden with studies in colonial administration. August 25. H.R. Rookmaaker, Senior marries Theodora Catharina Heitink.

1912 November 28. Theodora Catharina Rookmaaker, H.R.R.'s sister, born.

1912 January 30. Francis A. Schaeffer born.

1914 March 3. Henrietta Christina Rookmaaker, H.R.R.'s sister, born.

1915 August 15. Anna Marie (Anky) Huitker, H.R.R.'s wife, born in Sindanglaoet, Indonesia.

1919 May 10. Hendrika Beatrix (Riki) Spetter, H.R.R.'s fiancée, born.

1920 The Rookmaaker family returns to The Hague for H.R.R., Senior to pursue further studies in colonial administration.

1922 February 27. Henderik Roelof Rookmaaker born in The Hague.

1924 The Rookmaaker family resumes living in the Dutch Indies.

1927 H.R. Rookmaaker, Senior goes on an expedition to capture twelve Komodo dragons on Rintja in the Dutch Indies. H.R. Rookmaaker identifies a new species of frog (*Oreophryne rookmaakeri*).

1929 H.R. Rookmaaker, Senior becomes Assistent-Resident at Lho Semaweh (Lhokseumawe) on the north coast of Aceh in Sumatra, Dutch Indies.

1930 H.R. Rookmaaker identifies a new species of shell creature (*Xesta rookmaakeri*).

1931 The Rookmaaker family returns to The Hague for a year's leave.

1932 H.R.R. living once again in the Dutch Indies.

1936 H.R. Rookmaaker, Senior retires to The Hague due to ill health. H.R.R. is becoming an avid and discriminating collector of recorded African-American music.

1937 H.R. Rookmaaker, Senior's official Residency in the Dutch Indies terminated. **1938** H.R.R. is a midshipman (*adelborst*) at the Royal Netherlands Naval College at Den Helder. **1940** H.R.R. is engaged to Hendrika Beatrix (Riki) Spetter. May 10. The German occupation of the Netherlands. **1941** March 4. H.R.R. arrested for possession of anti-German literature and held in Scheveningen Prison in The Hague until December. **1942** April. H.R.R., as a commissioned officer, ordered by the Nazis to Breda and immediately incarcerated and transferred to a POW camp at Langwasser near Nuremberg. August 18. Riki Spetter is last seen at Westerbork. September 30. Riki Spetter dies at Auschwitz. (A fact H.R.R. never knew during his lifetime.) By the autumn, H.R.R. incarcerated at Stanislau (today Ivano Frankivsk) in western Ukraine. Japanese invasion of Dutch East Indies. **1943** H.R.R. meets J.P.A. Mekkes in Stanislau POW camp in late summer. September 19. H.R.R. dedicates to Riki Spetter his study of the Old Testament prophets, *Betreffende de Profetie*. **1944** February H.R.R. transferred to a POW camp at Neubrandenburg in northern Germany. **1945** January 31. H.R. Rookmaaker, Senior dies of a heart attack in The Hague. May 5. Liberation of the Netherlands. May 8. Armistice in Europe. Summer. H.R.R. makes his way back to The Hague. August 17. Indonesian independence declared. September 2. Armistice in the Pacific. **1947** H.R.R. founds the Vereniging van Gereformeerde Studenten te Amsterdam (VGSA). H.R.R. is engaged to Anky Huitker. **1948** August. H.R.R. meets Francis Schaeffer in Amsterdam. **1949** H.R.R. passes his *kandidaats* examination (equivalent to a Bachelor's degree). June 1. H.R.R. and Anna Marie (Anky) Huitker married at Amsterdam. H.R.R. starts writing art criticism for *Trouw*, a daily newspaper. **1950** July 15. Henderik Roelof Rookmaaker, son of Hans and Anky Rookmaaker, is born in Amsterdam. **1953** February 21. Leendert Cornelis (Kees) Rookmaaker, son of Hans and Anky Rookmaaker, is born in Amsterdam. **1954** August 26. Maria Helena (Marleen) Rookmaaker, daughter of Hans and Anky Rookmaaker, is born in Amsterdam. **1955** February. Francis and Edith Schaeffer threatened with expulsion from Switzerland. The inauguration of the L'Abri Fellowship. Summer. The Rookmaakers and their three children spend six weeks with the Schaeffers in Switzerland. **1956** H.R.R. stops writing for *Trouw* and turns his focus full-time to obtaining a doctorate in art history at the University of Amsterdam. **1957** H.R.R. begins teaching at the University of Leiden. The Rookmaaker family moves from Amsterdam to Leiden. **1958** Hans and Anky formalize their connection with the Schaeffers as the representatives of L'Abri Fellowship in the Netherlands.

1959 July 7. H.R.R. receives his doctorate from the University of Amsterdam.

1960 Publication of *Jazz, Blues, Spirituals* (Zomer & Keuning).

1961 H.R.R. makes his first visit to the United States and Canada on a Dutch government grant to research the teaching of art history in North America.

1964 H.R.R. is invited to be professor of art history at The Free University of Amsterdam. The Rookmaaker family moves from Leiden to Diemen, near Amsterdam.

1965 May 28. H.R.R. gives his inaugural address, "The Artist as a Prophet?" as professor of art history at The Free University of Amsterdam.

1967 H.R.R. begins traveling regularly to Great Britain through links with L'Abri Fellowship and Inter-Varsity Fellowship (now UCCF).

1968 Anky Rookmaaker founds Redt een Kind (Save a Child), an organization to support orphans and poor children in India and Africa.

1970 H.R.R. publishes *Modern Art and the Death of a Culture* (IVP) H.R.R. begins traveling regularly to North America after teaching at a summer school at Regent College (Vancouver, British Columbia, Canada). December 20. Malcolm Muggeridge makes *Modern Art and the Death of a Culture* one of his *Observer* Books of the Year.

1971 Dutch L'Abri is founded. July 12. Theodora Catharina Rookmaaker, H.R.R.'s mother, dies in The Hague.

1975 Hans and Anky Rookmaaker move to Ommeren.

1977 March 13. H.R.R. dies in Ommeren. March 16. H.R.R. buried at Eck en Wiel.

1984 May 15. Francis A. Schaeffer dies in Rochester, Minnesota, USA.

1987 J.P.A. Mekkes dies.

1989 Theodora Catharina (Door) Haver Droeze, elder sister of H.R.R., dies.

2002 Henrietta Christina (Hannie) Rotgans, younger sister of H.R.R., dies.

2003 February 10. Anky Rookmaaker, widow of H.R.R., dies at Hardenberg.

APPENDIX II:
SOURCES

NOTES TO PREFACE

The late Linette Martin wrote a brief study of the life of H.R. Rookmaaker shortly after his death, entitled *Hans Rookmaaker: A Biography* (London: Hodder & Stoughton; Downers Grove: InterVarsity Press, 1979). Until now this is the only book-length biography that has been written on him. Recently Graham Birtwistle has written a succinct entry on "Henderik Roelof Rookmaaker (1922–1977)" in *Biographical Dictionary of Evangelicals*, edited by Timothy Larsen (Downers Grove and Leicester: Inter-Varsity Press, 2003), pp. 563–565. Birtwistle has also contributed an essay on "H.R. Rookmaaker: The Shaping of his Thought" to the first volume of the *Complete Works* (CW, 1:xv–xxxiii). Jeremy S. Begbie's *Voicing Creation's Praise* (Edinburgh: T. & T. Clark, 1991), pp. 127–141 offers a perspective on Rookmaaker's aesthetic as it relates to the Neo-Calvinist tradition. A list of writings commenting on the work and thought of H.R.R. is included in this volume (also see *CW*, 6:434–446).

Primary documents for the life and work of Hans Rookmaaker that have been consulted extensively in preparation for this biography include: *The Complete Works of Hans R. Rookmaaker*, Vols. 1–6, edited by Marleen Hengelaar-Rookmaaker (Carlisle, UK: Piquant, 2002–2003), which were in the process of being edited as I was writing; Hans Rookmaaker Papers in the Special Collections of the Buswell Memorial Library, Wheaton College, Wheaton, Illinois, USA; papers, photographs, letters, official documents, annual appointment agendas, in the possession of the Rookmaaker family. In the interests of readability, liberty has been taken to make minor stylistic changes to some of the letters without changing the meaning. From 1970 to 1977 I had serious and sustained personal conversations with H.R.R. in Vancouver, Seattle, Amsterdam, Eck en Wiel (Netherlands), Lausanne, Huémoz (Switzerland), Mittersill (Austria), London, and other locations in the UK. During this time I had the opportunity of hearing H.R.R. lecture in many different contexts. I have also had extensive personal communication with members of the Rookmaaker family and a multitude of his former students, friends, colleagues, associates, and others who have been greatly influenced by him.

NOTES TO CHAPTER 1: IMPACT

The American Bible Society Gallery is located in mid-Manhattan (1865 Broadway, New York, NY 10023; www.americanbible.org/gallery). On the 2000 exhibition of images of Christ at the National Gallery, see Gabriel Finaldi et al., *The Image of Christ* (London: National Gallery Company Ltd, 2000), a catalog of the exhibition; Neil MacGregor with Erika Langmuir, *Seeing Salvation: Images of Christ in Art* (London: BBC, 2000); and "Nigel Halliday Talks to Neil MacGregor," *Third Way* (March 2000), pp. 17–21. On the development of contemporary Christian rock music, see John J. Thompson, *Raised By Wolves: The Story of Christian Rock & Roll* (Toronto: ECW, 2000). See the web sites of Christians in the Visual Arts: www.civa.org; *Image: A Journal of the Arts & Religion*, www.imagejournal.org; Christelijke Academie voor de Beeldende Kunsten/CABK, Kampen, www.huygens.nl/21000_frame.htm; and Leith School of Art, Edinburgh, www.leithschoolofart.co.uk.

Sources of information on the life and travels of Rookmaaker in this chapter include his annual appointment agendas, letters, and papers in the Special Collections at Wheaton College and in the possession of the Rookmaaker family. His book *Jazz, Blues, Spirituals* was originally written in Dutch (Wageningen: Zomer & Keuning, 1960) but is now available in English in CW (2:157–311). The quote from Tony Wales is from Hans's obituary, "H.R. Rookmaaker," *Third Way* (1/6 [24 March 1977]), p. 10. The review by Michael Shepherd is from the British journal *Art News* in 1971; I have a copy of the review with a note from H.R.R. indicating the source, but I have been unable to locate the exact issue and page number. Muggeridge lists *Modern Art and the Death of a Culture* as one of his four nominations for Books of the Year for *The Observer* (20 December 1970), p. 17; see also *Esquire*, 75 (March 1971), p. 16.

The quotations from Rookmaaker on "the new art" and "new vision of humanity" come from his essay "Commitment in Art" (originally published in *Art and the Public Today* [Huémoz-sur-Ollon: L'Abri Fellowship Foundation, 1968], pp. 5–21; CW, 5:188–203). H.R.R.'s study on Gauguin was published as *Synthetist Art Theories* (Amsterdam: Swets and Zeitlinger, 1959); rev. ed. published as *Gauguin and 19th Century Art Theory* (Amsterdam: Swets and Zeitlinger, 1972); CW, 1:3–227. The quotation from Nicholas Wolterstorff is from his article "On Looking at Paintings: A Look at Rookmaaker," *Reformed Journal* (February 1972), pp. 11–15. Information from Alva Steffler is based on personal communication with the author (November 16, 2002). J. I. Packer dubbed H.R.R. "the pipe-puffing pundit of Amsterdam" in "All That Jazz," *Christianity Today* 30/18 (December 12, 1986), p. 15. Michael Shepherd (in his review quoted above) described him as "the Dutch Kenneth Clark." On Decimal Index of Art of the Low Countries (DIAL)/Iconclass), see www.iconclass.nl. F.F. Bruce's comments are from his article "Regent College, Vancouver," *The Witness* (November 1970), pp. 418–419. David McKenna's letter to H.R.R. is in Special Collections, Wheaton College. Testimonials of a housewife and businessman were oral comments to me by Regent College Summer School students.

NOTES TO CHAPTER 2: CHILDHOOD

Information contained in this chapter is based on extensive interviews with members of the Rookmaaker family and review of family papers and photographs. On a visit to Indonesia in 1981, I verified some details of H.R.R, Senior's administrative tenure in the Dutch East Indies by consulting with the authorities in Jakarta who were then the custodians of the documentation of the former colonial administration. I also used L. C. (Kees) Rookmaaker, "The Life of H.R. Rookmaaker (1887–1945), Pioneer of Nature Conservation in the Dutch East Indies," *Säugetierkundliche Mitteilungen* 41/1 (1998), pp. 2–6. Family sources date the birth of H.R.R., Senior in 1887; however, some government sources give the year of his birth as 1888.

NOTES TO CHAPTER 3: YOUTH

The elder H.R.R.'s attitude toward churchgoing was narrated in a chapel talk by Hans Rookmaaker at Regent College in 1972. On this same occasion H.R.R. mentioned that he learned all his theology from Jelly Roll Morton! The substance of the material contained in this chapter was again obtained from conversations with the Rookmaaker family and from papers, letters, documents, and photographs in their possession. A short history of the Royal Netherlands Naval College at Den Helder is contained on their website: www.kim.nl/rnlnc/htm/rnlnchistory.htm.

NOTES TO CHAPTER 4: CONVERSION AND CALLING

Details for this chapter stem from personal letters of Hans Rookmaaker, his family, and Riki Spetter. Information concerning the internment camp at Langwasser near Nuremberg is found on the web site of Stadt Nürnberg: www.museen.nuernberg.de/english/reichsparteitag_e/pages/bauten_e.html. Information concerning the movement of Dutch prisoners from the POW camp at Colditz Castle to Stalag 371 at Stanislau (Ivano Frankivsk, Ukraine) in June 1943 came from www.geocities.com/schlosscolditz/colditz.html. L. Martin and others have incorrectly located Stanislau in Poland. Even today Stanislau is the German identification of Ivano Frankivsk. The four long quotations from Hans concerning his internment are from his reflections on the history of the Cosmonomic Idea (see *CW*, 2:10–12). The original manuscripts of "*Betreffende de Profetie*" and "*Aesthetica*" written in prison are in the Special Collections at Wheaton College. The former document is found in *CW*, 6:91–119 as "Prophecy in the Old and New Testaments: God's Way with Israel." The Bible Rookmaaker used was the so-called "Utrecht Translation" by H. Th. Obbink and A. M. Brouwer in 1942. "*Aesthetica*" was first published in two parts in *Philosophia Reformata* (1946–1947) and is found in *CW*,

2:24–79 as "Sketch for an Aesthetic Theory based on the Philosophy of the Cosmonomic Idea." Herman Dooyeweerd's major philosophical work that gave Rookmaaker a framework for his work as a Christian scholar is the three-volume *De Wijsbegeerte der Wetsidee* (1935–1936), which was later expanded and translated into English as *A New Critique of Theoretical Thought*, 3 volumes (Philadelphia: Presbyterian and Reformed, 1969). On Dooyeweerd, see J. Begbie, *Voicing Creation's Praise*, pp. 106–126. The collected works of Dooyeweerd are being translated into English and published in two multivolume series under the general editorship of D.F.M. Strauss through the Dooyeweerd Centre at Redeemer University College in Ancaster, Ontario, Canada and published by Mellen Press. For information about the publications, visit the web site of the Dooyeweerd Centre: www.redeemer.on.ca/dooyeweerdcentre.

The history and names of the variety of Reformed churches in the Netherlands are confusing even to those who read Dutch. Rookmaaker found his spiritual home with a group of congregations that had broken away from the Gereformeerde Kerken in Nederland (GKN), founded by Abraham Kuyper and associates near the end of the nineteenth century, in 1944 to form the Gereformeerde Kerken (Vrijgemaakt, GK(v)). In 1966–1967 the GK(v) experienced its own schism, leading to the founding of the Reformed Churches (Liberated, Unconnected), today the Netherlands Reformed Churches (NGK). Rookmaaker sided with the NGK, which has close links with the Christian Reformed Churches in the USA and Canada. See *The Reformed Family Worldwide*, ed. Jean-Jacques Bauswein and Lukas Vischer (Grand Rapids, Mich.: Eerdmans, 1999), pp. 383–394. Roel Kuiper and Marleen Hengelaar-Rookmaaker were helpful in clarifying the date and details of the schism.

NOTES TO CHAPTER 5: FAMILY AND CAREER

Details for this chapter are dependent on personal letters, papers, documents, and oral information from Hans and Anky Rookmaaker and their family. On the liberation of Neubrandenburg, see www.aiipowmia.com/wwii/wwiiwkgrp.html. On Rookmaaker's intensive study of the biblical prophets and also the work of Dooyeweerd and the Philosophy of the Cosmonomic Idea, see notes on Chapter 4 above. My last conversation with Hans's sister, Hannie Rotgans, took place in July 2001. See also notes on Chapter 4 above on the Reformed Church. For Rookmaaker's earliest work on aesthetics, see CW, 2:24–79. Much information concerning Anky Rookmaaker and her family is found in her chapter, "Lifting Up Holy Hands," in Lane T. Dennis, ed., *Francis Schaeffer: Portraits of the Man and His Work* (Wheaton, Ill.: Crossway Books, 1986), pp. 153–162. On Castle Eerde and the story of Krishnamurti, see www.nevenzel.com/eerde.htm. Information concerning the date and place of Riki Spetter's death was obtained from the Center for Research on Dutch Jewry at the Hebrew University of Jerusalem; see http://www.snunit.k12.il/sachlav/dutch/maineng/search.html. The quotation from Nobel Prize winner Czeslaw Milosz is from his book *The Land of Ulro* (New York: Farrar, Straus and Giroux, 1984), p. 152. Reference to "'personal knowledge' in the Polanyian sense" refers to Michael Polanyi's classic work *Personal Knowledge: Towards a Post-Critical Philosophy* (New York: Harper & Row, 1964). On the work of Dooyeweerd, see notes on Chapter 4 above.

I am indebted to Marleen Hengelaar-Rookmaaker for information on the history of the VGSA. Interestingly enough, she was the first woman president of the group when she was a student at the University of Amsterdam. It is also where she met her husband, Albert Hengelaar. On the International Council of Christian Churches, see *The Reformed Family Worldwide*, pp. 705–706; and D. K. Larsen, "Carl McIntire (1906–2002)," in

Biographical Dictionary of Evangelicals, pp. 393–395. On Francis and Edith Schaeffer and the work of L'Abri Fellowship, see C. Duriez, "Francis August Schaeffer (1912–1984)," *Biographical Dictionary of Evangelicals*, pp. 582–585; and Lane T. Dennis, ed., *Francis Schaeffer: Portraits of the Man and His Work*. The majority of Rookmaaker's exhibition reviews for *Trouw* are contained in CW, 1:229–361, but some are also included in CW, 4:461–479 and CW, 5:361–379.

Detailed bibliographical information on Rookmaaker's doctoral dissertation, *Synthetist Art Theories* (1959); rev. ed., *Gauguin and 19th Century Art Theory* (1972); CW, 1:3–227 is contained in notes to Chapter 1. On van Regteren Altena, see the electronic *A Biographical Dictionary of Historians, Museum Directors and Scholars of Art* (DAH); www.lib.duke.edu/lilly/artlibry/dah/regterna.htm. Graham Birtwistle's essay is found in CW, 1:xv–xxxiii. On the De Stijl movement, see H. L. C. Jaffé, *De Stijl, 1917–1931: The Dutch Contribution to Modern Art* (Amsterdam: Meulenhoff, 1956; repr. 1986). See Jaffé's obituary of H.R.R. in *Lier en Boog* (January 1978), p. 82. Jan Bialostocki's comments on van de Waal appear in his review of van de Waal's *Drie eeuwen vaderlandsche geschied-uitbeelding, 1500–1800: Een iconologische studie* (1952), in *The Art Bulletin*, 52 (1971), p. 264. On van de Waal, see DAH: www.lib.duke.edu/lilly/artlibry/dah/vandewaalh.htm and R.H. Fuchs, "Henri van de Waal, 1910–1972," in *Simiolus*, 6/1 (1972/73), pp. 5–7. On the RKD, see www.rkd.nl/frame-e.htm. On DIAL, see notes to Chapter 1. Information concerning Seerveld's and Schaeffer's writing to H.R.R.'s dissertation committee is contained in letters in the Special Collections at Wheaton College. For information on Redt een Kind (Save a Child), see www.redteenkind.org/en/.

NOTES TO CHAPTER 6: FRIENDSHIPS

On Mekkes, see "Bij het sterven van prof. Dr. J.P.A. Mekkes," *Nederlands Dagblad* (29 July 1987). On Vollenhoven, the colleague and brother-in-law of Dooyeweerd, see "Vollenhoven, Scriptural Philosophy, and Christian Higher Education" by John H. Kok; http://home.planet.nl/~srw/vollen/volkok.htm. On Schaeffer, see notes to Chapter 5 above. On Abraham Kuyper, see J.D. Bratt in *Biographical Dictionary of Evangelicals*, pp. 351–354; Peter S. Heslam, *Creating a Christian Worldview: Abraham Kuyper's Lectures on Calvinism* (Grand Rapids, Mich.: Eerdmans, 1998); and *Kuyper Reconsidered: Aspects of His Life and Work*, ed. Cornelis van der Kooi and Jan de Bruijn (Amsterdam: VU Uitgeverij, 1999). Kuyper's 1898 Stone Lectures at Princeton Theological Seminary were published in Dutch and English in 1889 (Amsterdam, London, Edinburgh, and New York). Since 1931, Eerdmans has had the copyright for the English edition of *Lectures on Calvinism* and has kept the book in print until today. On the various American Presbyterian groups to which Schaeffer was connected, see *Reformed Family Worldwide*, pp. 522, 532, 534, 537. On the spiritual hunger of the West in the 1960s, see Camille Paglia, "Cults and Cosmic Consciousness: Religious Vision in America in the 1960s," *Arion* (Winter 2003); www.bu.edu/arion/paglia_cults00.htm. On the Dutch L'Abri, see www.labri.nl/ and www.labri.nl/home_en.htm. On Cornelius Van Til, see J.M. Frame in *Biographical Dictionary of Evangelicals*, pp. 682–684. Van Swigchem wrote a brief history of the Department of Art History of the Free University in 2001, to which I was kindly given access courtesy of Graham Birtwistle. Information about L'Abri, the Schaeffers, and the Rookmaakers comes from correspondence in Special Collections at Wheaton College as well as L'Abri family letters in the possession of the Rookmaaker family. Comments of Rookmaaker concerning Schaeffer in his inaugural address are included in the introduction to *Art and the Public Today*, p. 3; CW, 5:167. Rookmaaker's *Kunst en*

Amusemusement (Kampen: J.H. Kok, 1962) is translated into English as "Art and Entertainment," *CW*, 3:1–131. Information concerning Seerveld and Rookmaaker is based on personal conversations and letters in Special Collections at Wheaton College. *Modern Art and the Death of a Culture* (London: Inter-Varsity Press, 1970) is found in *CW*, 5:1–164. Both David Alexander and H.R.R. expressed warm appreciation for their collaborative relationship. In fact, in recognition of the fact that Alexander had been so helpful in the copy-editing of his English style, Rookmaaker went so far as to suggest that his name should be included on the title page, but Alexander demurred. Rookmaaker confessed, "He greatly improved my English style while retaining my voice!" Rookmaaker's "provocative" quote on Christian standards comes from L. Martin, p. 146. "Letter to a Christian Artist" is now in *CW*, 3:209–213. The quotation, "How can you say modern art is ugly when you worship the Lord in a building painted like this?" is taken from *Arts & Minds: The Story of Nigel Goodwin* by David Porter (London: Houghton and Stoughton, 1993), p. 109. Quotes on van Goyen and a student come from Linette Martin, p. 138.

NOTES TO CHAPTER 7: PASSIONS

As we move into the era of more recent history, more and more of the details are dependent on personal interviews, informal conversations, and personal correspondence (both e-mail and "snail mail") with participants in the story, in addition to the usual written documents contained in the Rookmaaker Archives of the Special Collections at Wheaton College and in the possession of the Rookmaaker family.

Also, J. H. van den Berg, *Metabletica, of Leer der veranderingen: beginselen van een historische psychologie* (Nijkerk: Callenbach, 1956); English text, *The Changing Nature of Man* (New York: Norton, 1961). The phrase "theology through the arts" represents a movement that has been spearheaded by Jeremy S. Begbie; see www.theoarts.org. On art monuments as historical documents, see Margaret R. Miles, *Image as Insight: Visual Understanding in Western Christianity and Secular Culture* (Boston: Beacon Press, 1985). On Groen van Prinsterer, see Harry Van Dyke, ed. and trans., *Groen Van Prinsterer's Lectures on Unbelief and Revolution* (Jordan Station, Ont., Canada: Wedge Publishing Foundation, 1989), pp. 39–83. Translation is available in electronic form at http://capo.org/gvp.htm. The quote from Kuyper is from his *Lectures on Calvinism* (Grand Rapids, Mich.: Eerdmans, [1931] 1976), pp. 165–166. Experience and quotation from David Muir was passed on to me in a communication from Elria Kwant (April 2003). The recollection of Sharon Gallagher was communicated to me personally (March 2003). For a contemporary discussion on the visual arts in Calvinism, see Paul Corby Finney, ed., *Seeing Beyond the Word: Visual Arts and the Calvinist Tradition* (Grand Rapids, Mich.: Eerdmans, 1999).

NOTES TO CHAPTER 8: LEGACY

I have had more than one occasion in recent years to be in personal contact with or to have communication from the majority of the individuals mentioned in this chapter. Some I have known for a considerable amount of time. I have expressed appreciation in my acknowledgments to those who have provided me with helpful information; hence, it would be too tedious to repeat the names of these individuals in the notes. Rather, I will seek to offer literary documentation of a few specific details and will reserve the bulk of the space here to list web sites with which the individuals and organizations mentioned are associated. In many cases the interested reader will be able to learn a great deal about the work of the people and groups that have in some manner been influenced by the life and vision of Hans Rookmaaker.

Comments by Peter Smith are from a review of Rookmaaker's *Complete Works*, Volumes 1–2 for *ArtsMedia*, 3 (Autumn 2002), conveyed to me in electronic form. The observations by Rachel Smith were made in a personal communication at the Christians in the Visual Arts biennial conference (June 2003). Information from and concerning Graham Birtwistle has been by way of recent e-mail and fax exchanges as well as personal conversations since we were students in England in the late 1960s. Rookmaaker's positive evaluation of the art of Georges Rouault is in *CW*, 5:236–239. Information on John Walford is from articles in the *Wheaton Record* (September 25, 1981) and a Wheaton alumni magazine 15/6 (2002), pp. 20–21; an audiotape produced during a visit of Anky Rookmaaker and Marleen Hengelaar-Rookmaaker to the Wheaton College campus (1985); and personal communication. Rookmaaker corresponded with Panofsky about his work on Michelangelo (*CW*, 4:73-101), met Frederick Hartt in Italy, received a visit from Bialostocki in Amsterdam, and corresponded with Nochlin and Chipp. The interview by art history students at the Free University is found in *CW*, 3:496–501. H.R.R.'s use of the example of Descartes as an illustration of tolerance and intellectual freedom in the Calvinist heritage is found in his Westminster discussions on television and film (*CW*, 3:455-459). Susan Snell, "History of CA," (2000), www.continentals.nl/ downloads/HistoryCA.pdf, gives an overview of Christian Artists Association. *Reality Revisited by Six Dutch Painters*, by Hans van Seventer and JoAnn van Seventer (Zwiggelte: The Zwiggelte Group, 1982) documents the early work of Dutch artists influenced by Rookmaaker. The quotation from Mary Leigh Morbey is from an e-mail message (June 2003). On Sempangi's early work, see his book *A Distant Grief* (Glendale: G/L Publications, 1979). For Kwame Bediako's vision, see his *Theology & Identity: The Impact of Culture Upon Christian Thought in the Second Century and Modern Africa* (Oxford: Regnum Books, 1992). Peter Heslam's comment is from his essay "A Theology of the Arts: Kuyper's Ideas on Art and Religion," in *Kuyper Reconsidered* (Amsterdam: VU Uitgeverij, 1999), p. 25. On Nigel Goodwin, see the biography by David Porter (mentioned in notes to Chapter 6 above). Also, David and Tricia Porter, *Over the Bent World* (Carlisle: Paternoster Press, 1999). The comment from Paul Martin is from a personal letter to the author by Philip Archer (May 2003). Some of the information concerning musicians influenced by Rookmaaker was obtained from Thompson's *Raised By Wolves* (see notes to Chapter 1); others come from personal knowledge.

Web-site Links for People and Organizations Mentioned in Chapter 8

Names are listed in the order in which they are mentioned in the narrative. I was unable to find a web link for the people mentioned but not listed.

Peter Smith, artist and educator, Kingston College, UK: www.kingston-college.ac.uk/d

Rachael Smith, art historian, Taylor University: www.tayloru.edu/upland/ academics/departments/visualarts.html

Graham Birtwistle, art historian, Free University of Amsterdam: www.vu.nl

John Walford, art historian, Wheaton College: www.wheaton.edu/ homeArt.html

Paul Martin, artist and educator, Leith School of Art: www.theartroom.net and www.leithschoolofart.co.uk

Sandra Martin, artist and educator, Leith School of Art: www.leithschoolofart.co.uk

Martin Rose, artist: www.theartroom.net

Kate Rose, artist: www.theartroom.net

Meryl and Malcolm Doney, authors and impresarios, The Art Room: www.theartroom.net

James Romaine, author and art historian: http://squarehalobooks.com/oog.htm

Ned Bustard, artist and publisher, Square Halo Books: www.square HaloBooks.com

Marc de Klijn, artist and author: www.solcon.nl/langeveld/keerpunt/k/klijn-marc-de-schilder.htm

Hans and JoAnn van Seventer, publishers, writers and producers: www.defilmderedding.nl/content/aanzet.html

Nederlandse Christelijke Radio: http://info.omroep.nl/ncrv/home?nav=ijcgFsHtGPJqK

Evangelische Omroep: www.eo.nl/home/html/home.jsp

Christelijk Academie voor de Beeldende Kunsten/CABK: http://www.huygens.nl/21000_frame.htm

Christian Artists Vereniging voor Beeldende Kunsten (CABK): www.continentals.nl

Christian Artists Association (Kunstenbond-CNV or CA): www.continentals.nl

Leen La Riviére, impresario: www.continentals.nl

Jan van Loon, artist: www.stoneart.nl/realisten/vanloon.html

Henk Helmantel, artist: www.helmantel.nl

Rein Pol, artist: www.stoneart.nl/realisten/pol.html

Jan van der Scheer, artist: www.galeries.nl/mnkunstenaar.asp?artistnr=4314&vane=1&sessionti=340898117

Jan Zwaan, artist: www.galeriebakker.nl/pages/kunstenaars/JanZwaan

Christelijk Studiecentrum ICS: www.impactnetwerk.nl

International Fellowship of Evangelical Students (IFES): www.ifesworld.org/defaulthome.asp

Wim and Greta Rietkerk, senior staff, Dutch L'Abri: www.labri.nl

Pieter and Elria Kwant, publishers, Piquant: www.piquant.net

L'Abri International: www.labri.org

Swiss L'Abri: www.labri.org/switzerland.html

British L'Abri: www.labri.org/england.html

H. G. (Henk) Geertsema, philosopher, Vereniging voor Reformatorische Wijsbegeerte: http://home.planet.nl/~srw/home.htm

Mary Leigh Morbey, art historian, York University, Canada: www.edu.yorku.ca:8080/~mmorbey/home.htm

H. R. (Hans) Rookmaaker, rector, Christelijk Gymnasium Sorghvliet, The Hague: www.sorghvliet.demon.nl

L. C. (Kees) Rookmaaker, Special Advisor, International Rhino Foundation: www.rhinoresourcecenter.com/

Marleen Hengelaar-Rookmaaker, editor, LEV: www.labri.nl and www.piquant.net/PDFs/Rookmaaker_cat.pdf

Calvin Seerfeld, emeritus, Institute for Christian Studies: www.icscanada.edu/faculty/index.shtml and www.seerveld.com/tuppence.html

T. Grady Spires, emeritus, Gordon College: www.gordon.edu

Gordon College, Art Department: www.gordon.edu/academics/art/

Gordon College, Center for Christian Studies: www.gordon.edu/ccs

Christians in the Visual Arts: www.civa.org

Ted Prescott, artist and educator, Messiah College: www.messiah.edu/
departments/art/

Catherine Prescott, artist and educator, Messiah College: www.messiah.
edu/departments/art/

Bill Edgar, musician and theologian, Westminster Theological Seminary:
www.wts.edu/faculty/faculty-htstudies.html#edgar

Thena Ayres, educator, Regent College: www.regent-college.edu

William Dyrness, theologian, Brehm Center, Fuller Theological Seminary:
www.fuller.edu/brehmcenter/

Regent College Spring and Summer School Program: www.regent-college.edu

Ward and Laurel Gasque, educators: www.koinos.org

Hannah Main-van der Kamp, poet: www3.sympatico.ca/voxfeminarum/bios.html

Dal Schindell, artist and educator, Regent College: www.regent-college.edu

Roger Feldman, artist and educator, Seattle Pacific University:
www.spu.edu/depts/fpa/

Wayne Roosa, art historian, Bethel College (Minnesota): www.bethel.edu/
college/acad/dept/art.htm

Mary Ellen Ashcroft, educator, Bethel College (Minnesota): www.bethel.edu/
college/dept/english/faculty.html

Betty Spackman, artist and educator, Trinity Western University:
www.twu.ca/news/news_detail.asp?NewsID=241

Chris Anderson, Painting Fellow, New York Foundation for the Arts:
www.chrisandersonart.com and http://nyfa.org/nyfa_artists_detail.asp?pid=96

Bettina Clowney, artist and spiritual director: http://thegalleriesatmoore.org/
gmslide/search.cgi?code=2655

Lee Hendrix, curator of prints, J. Paul Getty Museum: www.getty.edu

Gerard Pas, artist: www.gerardpas.com

Sharon Gallagher, editor, *Radix* magazine: http://www.radixmagazine.com/

Kefa Sempangi, artist and Member of Parliament, Uganda: www.ambrosia
finearts.com/galleries/kefa_sempangi.html

Kwame Bediako, theologian, Akrofi-Christaller Memorial Centre, Ghana:
www.ocms.ac.uk/regnum/detail.asp?book_id=8

David and Ruth Hanson, educators, West Yorkshire School of Christian Studies:
www.wysocs.org.uk/why_wysocs.html

Nigel Goodwin, actor, Genesis Arts Trust: www.tradeandtryon.com/gat/

Sylvester Jacobs, photographer and educator: www.weeks-g.dircon.co.uk/
SylvesterJacobs.htm

Linette Martin, author (deceased): www.parable.com/nrb/item_1557253072.htm

Colin Duriez, author and publishing consultant: www.renew.org.uk/spck/cat/
author.php?3192

Arts Centre Group: www.artscentregroup.org.uk

Norman Stone, filmmaker: www.wheaton.edu/leamres/ARCSC/collects/
sc13/bio.htm

Murray Watts, theatre and film director and author: www.ridinglights.org

David Porter, author: www.porterfolio.com

Tricia Porter, photographer: www.porterfolio.com

London Institute for Contemporary Christianity: www.licc.org.uk

Third Way magazine: www.thirdway.org.uk

Greenbelt Arts Festival: www.greenbelt.org.uk

John Peck, pastor and promoter of the arts: www.greenbelt.org.uk

Philip Archer, artist and educator, Leith School of Art: www.the
artroom.net and www.leithschoolofart.co.uk

Theology Through the Arts, Cambridge and St Andrews: www.theolarts.org

Institute for Theology, Imagination and the Arts, University of St Andrews:
www.st-andrews.ac.uk/institutes/itia/index.htm

Jeremy Begbie, musician and theologian, Cambridge University:
www.theolarts.org/people.html

Ric Ashley, musician and educator, Northwestern University:
www.nici.kun.nl/mmm/persona/ashley/ashley.html

Garth Hewitt, musician: www.garthhewitt.com

Mark Heard, musician (deceased): www.mh.rru.com

Steve Turner, poet: www.lion-publishing.co.uk/authors/meet_steve_turner.htm

Steve Scott, author, Arts and Media Group, Warehouse Christian Ministries:
www.gaylen.com/resume/sresume.html

Eleanor DeLorme, lecturer and curator, Davis Museum, Wellesley College:
www.wellesley.edu/PublicAffairs/Profile/af/edelorme.html